SAVING THE TIGER

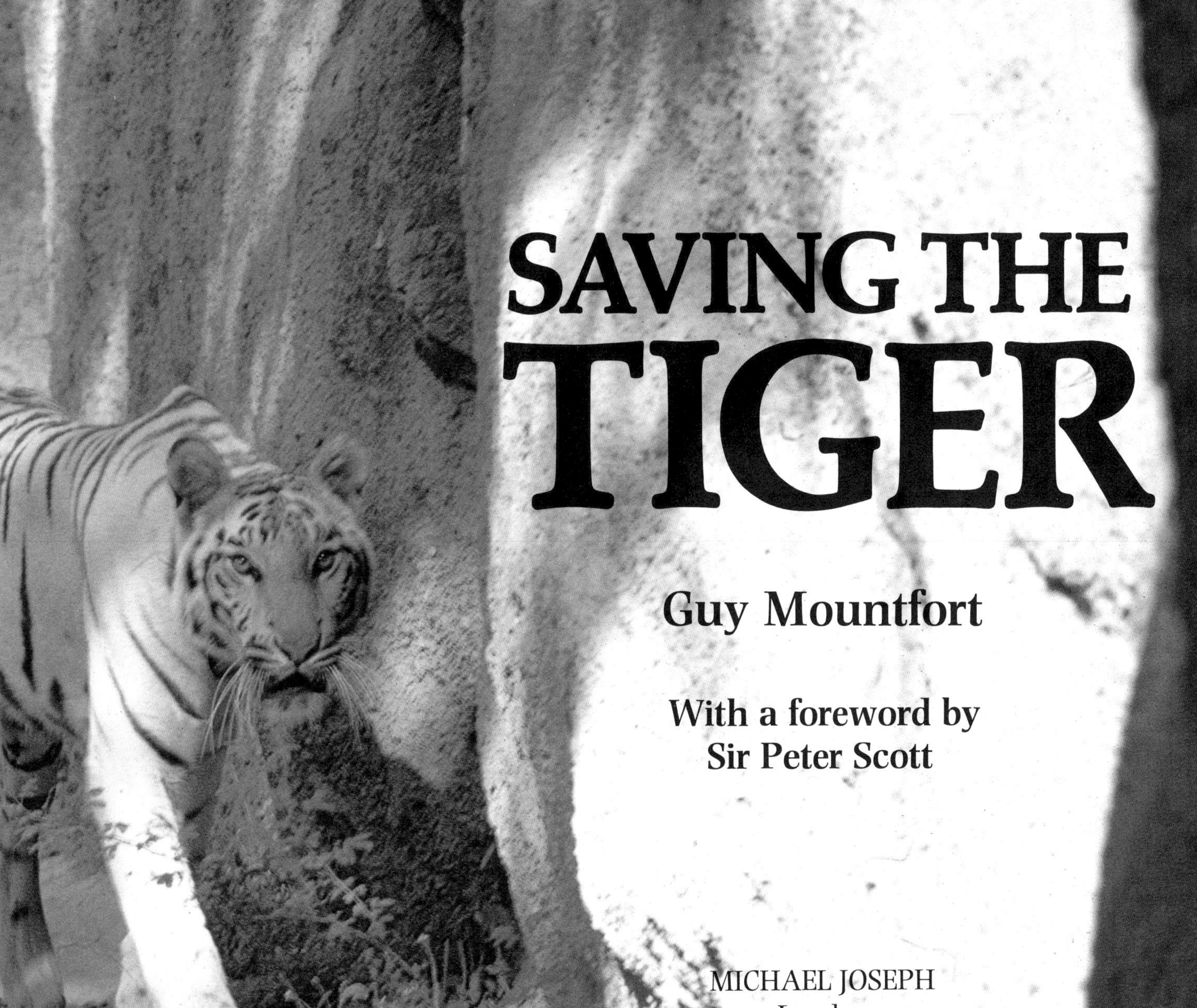

SAVING THE TIGER

Guy Mountfort

With a foreword by
Sir Peter Scott

MICHAEL JOSEPH
London

First published in Great Britain by Michael Joseph Ltd
44 Bedford Square,
London WC1

Reprinted 1983

This book was designed and produced by
John Calmann & Cooper Ltd

ISBN 0 7181 1991 6

Filmset in England by Southern Positives and Negatives
(SPAN), Lingfield, Surrey
Printed in Hong Kong by Dai Nippon

Previous spread: One of the rare white tigers of Rewa.

Contents

Foreword by Sir Peter Scott	page 7
Preface	8
Part I – THE LIFE OF THE TIGER	10
The species and its distribution	13
Food and methods of hunting	25
Territory and the telemetry project	37
Scent as a 'biochemical fingerprint'	45
Vocalization	46
Reproduction	50
Education of the cubs	56
Man-eating by tigers	59
Part II – THE DOWNFALL OF THE TIGER	68
Losses caused by hunting	70
Destruction of the tiger's habitat	77
Could the tiger be saved?	80
Part III – BACK FROM THE BRINK	89
India takes the initiative	91
'Operation Tiger' is launched	101
The tiger is saved	113
Selected Bibliography	118
Scientific names of the species	119
Acknowledgements	119
Index	120

Foreword

During a fund-raising tour for the World Wildlife Fund in Florida early in 1972, Guy Mountfort gave details, in the course of a speech, of the catastrophic decline in the numbers of tigers, and proposed that a million dollars could and should be raised forthwith to prevent the extinction of this magnificent species. The proposal received immediate acclaim, although some of us sitting listening realized that a lot of work would be necessary before we could decide how such money might best be spent.

I think the instantaneous and enthusiastic response took even Guy by surprise. Operation Tiger was born with its eyes open and already running. It never looked back.

This book is about that Operation – saving the tiger. But why and for whom? There are of course ethical reasons – because wiping out a wonderful animal out of carelessness or ignorance must be morally wrong. But no less important is that allowing the tiger to become extinct in this generation would represent an irreversible loss to the next. Keeping the options open for future generations must be a basic principle for all civilized people. What they do with those options when the time comes will be up to them, but we can only hope they too will embrace the principle.

Operation Tiger is not only important for what it is doing for tigers. It is clear that the tiger's habitat must be saved, and that means protecting whole ecosystems of forest, with their hosts of interdependent plants and animals. All must be saved if the tiger at the top of the food pyramid is to survive. Thus Operation Tiger provides a perfect example of a well-known animal becoming the focal point of a campaign which has led to the overall conservation of many forest areas in Asia. When Guy Mountfort announced his idea in Palm Beach in 1972 he was making conservation history. The implementation of the Operation in India and other Asian countries, with the collaboration of the International Union for the Conservation of Nature and the World Wildlife Fund, has been one of the basic steps in the evolution of the World Conservation Strategy prepared by IUCN and WWF in association with UNEP, FAO and UNESCO and published in March 1980.

For all these reasons I am honoured to have been invited to contribute this foreword.

SIR PETER SCOTT

1. Of all the world's animals, the tiger is one of the most magnificent and most colourful. It is the dominant predator of Asia, fearing no other animal but man.

Preface

If a world-wide opinion poll could be taken to ascertain which wild animal was most popular and most easily recognized, the tiger would probably head the list. Almost everyone has seen tigers in a zoo or a circus. They appear on films, on television, in advertisements, in children's books, on coats of arms, regimental badges, even on the labels of beer cans and of dubious medicaments. Football and baseball teams and a famous British warship proudly bear the name 'Tiger'. It has in fact become a universal symbol for majesty and power.

Yet for all this, the number of people who have actually set eyes on a wild tiger in the forests of Asia is extremely small. Until very recent times the private life of the species had not been studied in close detail except in zoos. Books by tiger hunters of course proliferated during the last century, but in order to heighten the authors' prowess in the eyes of their readers these usually left a very misleading impression of the supposedly innate ferocity of the animals which had fallen to their guns. Such hunters gained their experience over the barrel of a gun and some were surprisingly ignorant about the domestic lives of tigers. Not until 1965 was a serious scientific attempt made to establish the true facts about the way tigers live, hunt and reproduce in a natural state. Other admirably well documented studies have been made since then and the gaps in our knowledge are gradually being closed.

Although I have studied tigers in India, Bangladesh and Nepal and am frankly enamoured of them, I make no claim to have added anything of importance to the work of the modern specialists. My involvement was chiefly in the world-wide effort which had to be made in order to prevent these magnificent animals from becoming extinct, a tragedy which in 1969 seemed almost inevitable. This effort was made by the World Wildlife Fund, of which I have been an International Trustee since its creation in 1961. 'Operation Tiger' was only one of some 2,850 conservation projects which this remarkable charitable foundation had completed by 1980. All were financed by donations from the general public of many nations, the total thus subscribed amounting by then to no less than £22 million ($53 million).

This book, which summarizes existing knowledge of the tiger's way of life, traces the causes of its near extermination by man and tells the story of how, at the eleventh hour, salvation was brought about and the tiger was saved for posterity. I hope readers will share my feeling that the enthusiasm with which a dozen Asian nations co-operated in this extremely difficult task was singularly encouraging. Certainly the fact that these impoverished Third World countries should be eager to contribute so substantially, to save what they regarded as part of their national heritage, was an inspiration to those of us from the West who shared the work with them. 'Operation Tiger' has, indeed, been justly described as one of the great conservation successes of modern times.

The question may be asked why it was so important to prevent the extinction of an animal which, after all, is a powerful and potentially dangerous carnivore, prone to kill domestic cattle and even people. I have attempted to answer this in some detail, because until we understand the full consequences of man's destruction of the natural world we shall continue, through ignorance or inertia, our present headlong course towards the eventual breakdown of our own biological life-support system. Whether we recognize it or not, the tiger is part of the intricate web of life on earth, on the maintenance of which our own survival depends.

I have listed in the Selected Bibliography the published works on which I have drawn in preparing this book. I acknowledge with gratitude the help I have received from the authors and from tiger experts such as Dr George Schaller, Professor Paul Leyhausen, Dr Dave Smith, Dr Charles McDougal, Mr Kailash Sankhala, Mr Arjan Singh, Mr Zafar Futehally and particularly Mr Peter Jackson, the Project Officer of 'Operation Tiger', who not only read the manuscript but provided many of the illustrations. To the countless people of many nations who responded to the World Wildlife Fund appeal for money to execute this great project, the whole world is indebted.

I thank Messrs Hutchinson and Messrs David & Charles for permission to include some paraphrased extracts from my books *Back from the Brink* and *Tigers* in this present volume. I was grateful to the late Mr John Calmann of John Calmann and Cooper Ltd., for his invitation to write the story of 'Operation Tiger'; also for his agreement that so glamorous a subject deserved to be lavishly illustrated in colour by the few wildlife photographers who have succeeded in obtaining pictures of the elusive tiger in its natural setting. This book in fact contains the most complete pictorial documentation yet assembled on the species.

The Life of the Tiger

'You will never forget your first sight of a wild tiger,' an old Indian hand had assured me. Having grown accustomed to lions and other spectacular wildlife in Africa I took this with a grain of salt; after all, I had seen plenty of tigers in zoos and knew what to expect. Yet when it happened I had to agree with him. I can remember every detail as though it were only yesterday.

I was riding a well trained elephant in the Kanha National Park in the Indian state of Madhya Pradesh. It was a glorious post-monsoon sunrise and the sal forest was vividly green with fresh foliage, from which colourful trumpets of hanging vines cascaded on all sides. Presently the heat would become oppressive, but at dawn the air was deliciously cool and my mahout still wore the protective head-shawl in which he had slept. We were descending a slope towards a stream, zigzagging between twenty-foot clumps of feathery bamboo. The elephant's huge feet made no sound in the lush grass and its trunk brushed aside the branches across our path.

The stream came into view and suddenly a magnificent tiger rose from a patch of dead grass, seized the 400-pound carcass of a young buffalo by the neck and walked away with it, without apparent effort, into a clump of bamboo. Seconds later it emerged and stood staring at us haughtily. The mahout spoke softly and our elephant halted, motionless. For a full minute the picture froze. Then the elephant, although accustomed to the sight of tigers, could not contain its dislike of them any longer and began a deep, subterranean rumbling. The tiger turned and at leisurely pace walked away to our right, circled behind us and passed again on our left, no more than thirty paces away. Ignoring our presence, it stopped to sniff a sunlit patch of bamboo and then, with an audible sigh, subsided gracefully against it, its feet towards us, blinking its amber eyes in the bright light. Still paying us no attention whatever, it licked one of its immense fore-paws, yawned cavernously and to my amazement began to doze. The click of my camera

2. A tiger setting out at dusk on a hunting expedition. Tigers are chiefly but not exclusively nocturnal.

shutter ended this entrancing incident and the tiger vanished into the undergrowth.

What impressed me most was the obvious difference between this tiger and any I had seen in captivity. Its brilliantly striped orange and black coat gleamed like satin, whereas most zoo tigers have dull fur. Its long, infinitely supple strides through the grass, with muscles rippling and bulging, seemed quite unlike the plodding gait of an animal confined to a steel and concrete cage. This tiger, I realized, was free and in the full splendour of a natural existence. Although I later saw many more wild tigers in other parts of Asia, I never forgot this first revelation. At that moment began what my friends called my obsession with tigers and my determination to ensure the survival of the species.

It was fortunate that I chose the Kanha for my first experience of tiger-watching. This long established and excellently managed reserve affords a better chance than any other for seeing tigers in daylight. They have forgotten what it was like to be shot at whenever they came across a man and now pay scant attention to elephant-borne tourists, providing that the latter keep quiet and motionless in their presence. I chose the Kanha not for this reason, however, but because it was there that my friend Dr George Schaller had conducted his eighteen-month intensive study of tigers. His remarkable book, *The Deer and the Tiger*, the first detailed story of the private life of the tiger, was based entirely on his observations in the wild.

Schaller dispelled many previous misconceptions about tigers and produced some fascinating new facts concerning their behaviour. Taking advantage of the open nature of the Kanha forest, which in many areas offers excellent facilities for observation, and scorning the belief that tigers are inherently dangerous animals, he followed them on foot or occasionally by elephant, day after day. On several occasions he found himself face to face with one, but these close encounters elicited no more than a warning growl. Once or twice a surprised tiger made a few hesitant bounds towards him, but invariably withdrew after this token demonstration. Only once did he have to climb a tree, after inadvertently arousing a sleeping tigress at a distance of only four feet.

Following Schaller's example, I never carried a gun during my own studies of tigers, except on one occasion when I spent a night in a *machan* (tree-hide) among some known man-eaters in the Sunderbans mangrove swamps of Bangladesh. Here the local authorities insisted that I should borrow a gun, although the precaution proved unnecessary. Despite all the stories told by hunters, the tiger is a good-tempered animal which can be studied like any other wild creature so long as reasonable care is taken.

Two other reliable books about tigers were published in 1974 and 1977. The first was by Kailash Sankhala, who played a leading part in the campaign to save the tiger in India. The second, by Dr Charles McDougal, was a fascinating account of five years of close study in the Royal Chitwan National Park in the Nepalese terai that added many new facts to our knowledge of the species.

3. A tiger resting at midday in the shade in the Kanha National Park in India.

The species and its distribution

Scientists generally divide the tiger species into eight geographical races, or subspecies, according to small differences in colouration, striping, size and shape of the skull. These are the Siberian, *Panthera tigris altaica*; the Chinese *P.t. amoyensis*; the Indo-Chinese *P.t. corbetti*; the Indian which, since it was the first to be described, is called the nominate race, *P.t. tigris*; the Caspian *P.t. virgata*; the Sumatran *P.t. sumatrae*; the Javan *P.t. sondaica*; and the Balinese *P.t. balica*. The species *Panthera tigris* is thought to have originated in the region of present-day Manchuria, probably during the Pliocene period, between seven and four and a half million years ago. Contrary to popular opinion, it is not descended from the prehistoric sabre-toothed tiger, whose nearest living relative is more likely to be the clouded leopard of Asia; this leopard has abnormally long canine teeth although these are puny compared with the eight-inch slashers of its supposed ancestor.

As succeeding millennia passed the moist warm climate of northern Asia became cooler and as the numbers and varieties of grazing and browsing hoofed animals increased, the tiger began to spread southwards, until eventually it occupied nearly all the sub-tropical and tropical parts of the continent where its prey was available. This gradual invasion took two routes. The first ran from China and Indo-China to India via Burma and then moved southwards through the Malayan peninsula and across land-bridges

4. (Below) *A captive Siberian tiger showing the characteristic ruffle around the cheeks of adults. The fur of this race is long and dense, in keeping with a cold climate.*

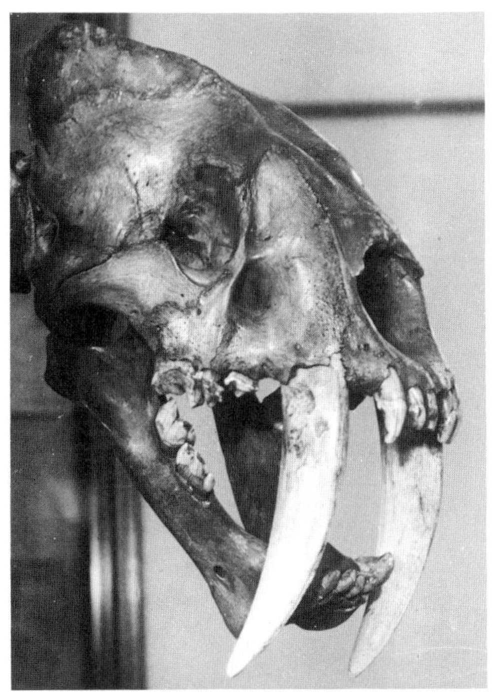

5. (Left) *A sabre-toothed tiger skull. The Smilodon or sabre-toothed tiger belonged to the now extinct genus Machairodus. It disappeared before the close of the Ice Age and was not the ancestor of today's tiger.*

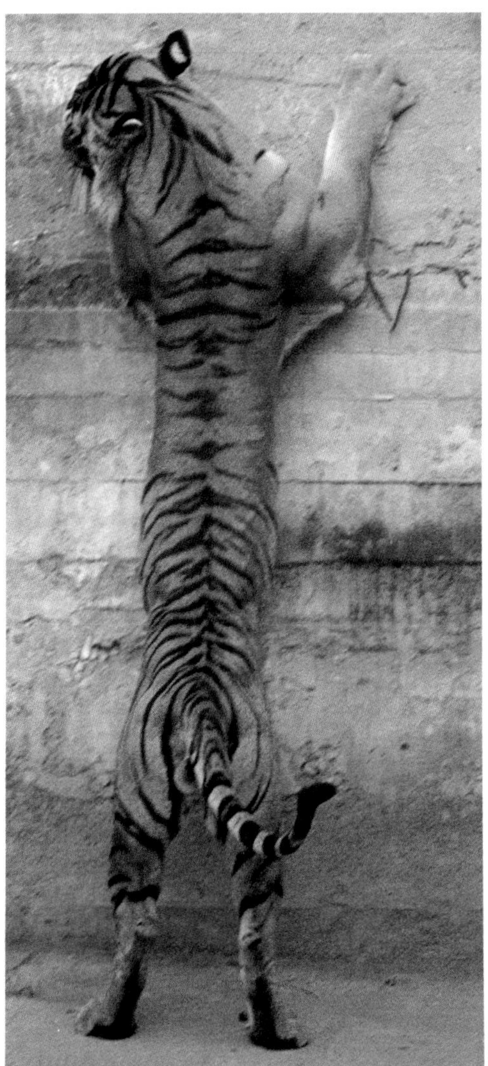

6. (Below) *A tiger stretching against a wall in a Chinese zoo. The photograph shows the thin hind legs of the tiger, its long abdomen, and powerful front legs.*

to Sumatra, Java and Bali, which later became islands. The second route skirted the high altitudes of Tibet, the Himalayas and the Pamirs and moved westwards through central Asia around the southern part of the Aral and Caspian Seas as far as Azerbaijan, northern Iran and Afghanistan and, eventually, eastern Turkey. Ceylon by then had become separated from India and was not colonized, whereas Pakistan had not yet become largely a desert region and tigers occupied the Indus valley until 1886.

Taking the present-day species as a whole, one can see considerable differences between the northern and southern races. The Siberian tiger is a massive animal, said to have reached a record length of 13 feet and a weight of well over 700 pounds. Such figures are, however, open to some doubt, according to whether the animal was measured by following the contours of the body or in a straight line between pegs, and whether or not its stomach still contained 50 pounds or so of recently eaten prey. The Siberian race has long, often rather shaggy fur, in keeping with a cold climate; the background colour is paler than that of the southern races.

Tigers of northern India average nine feet six inches long, one foot longer at maximum. An average male weighs 400–450 pounds. Females, as in the other races, are six to twelve inches smaller, weighing on average 300 pounds. Tigers in Nepal and Bhutan, although of the same sub-species, tend to be larger and heavier than those of northern India, the record length being eleven feet and the maximum weight 705 pounds, although both figures are exceptional.

In the extreme south of the tiger's range, adult Indonesian males are no more than nine feet long on average. The general colouration is dark, with narrower striping and slightly shorter fur than in the Indian or northern races. The skulls of the small Javan and Balinese tigers also differ in minor detail from those of the more northern races.

In general, then, it can be said that the tiger developed a gradual southward cline, from maximum to minimum average size and weight, from palest to darkest colouration and from longest to shortest fur, thus conforming to Bergmann's and Gloger's rules.*

The map on page 16 shows the approximate original ranges of the eight races of the tiger, compared with their present status. Information about the boundaries of earlier distribution is, of course, too scarce to be very reliable and in some instances must be little more than conjecture. The scale of the map is also too small to take into account areas of desert or other features that would exclude tigers. Nevertheless it is immediately evident that the tiger is a remarkably adaptable animal in so far as habitat is concerned. The Siberian race occurs in birch, scrub-oak and walnut thickets and its tracks have been seen in deep snow in cedar woods at a temperature of −34°C (−30°F). The Chinese race occurs in oak and poplar forests and in high

*Bergmann's Rule states that the races of warm-blooded animals in cool climates tend to be larger than their races in warm climates; Gloger's Rule that those in cool, dry areas tend to have paler pigmentation than their races in areas of high humidity and heat.

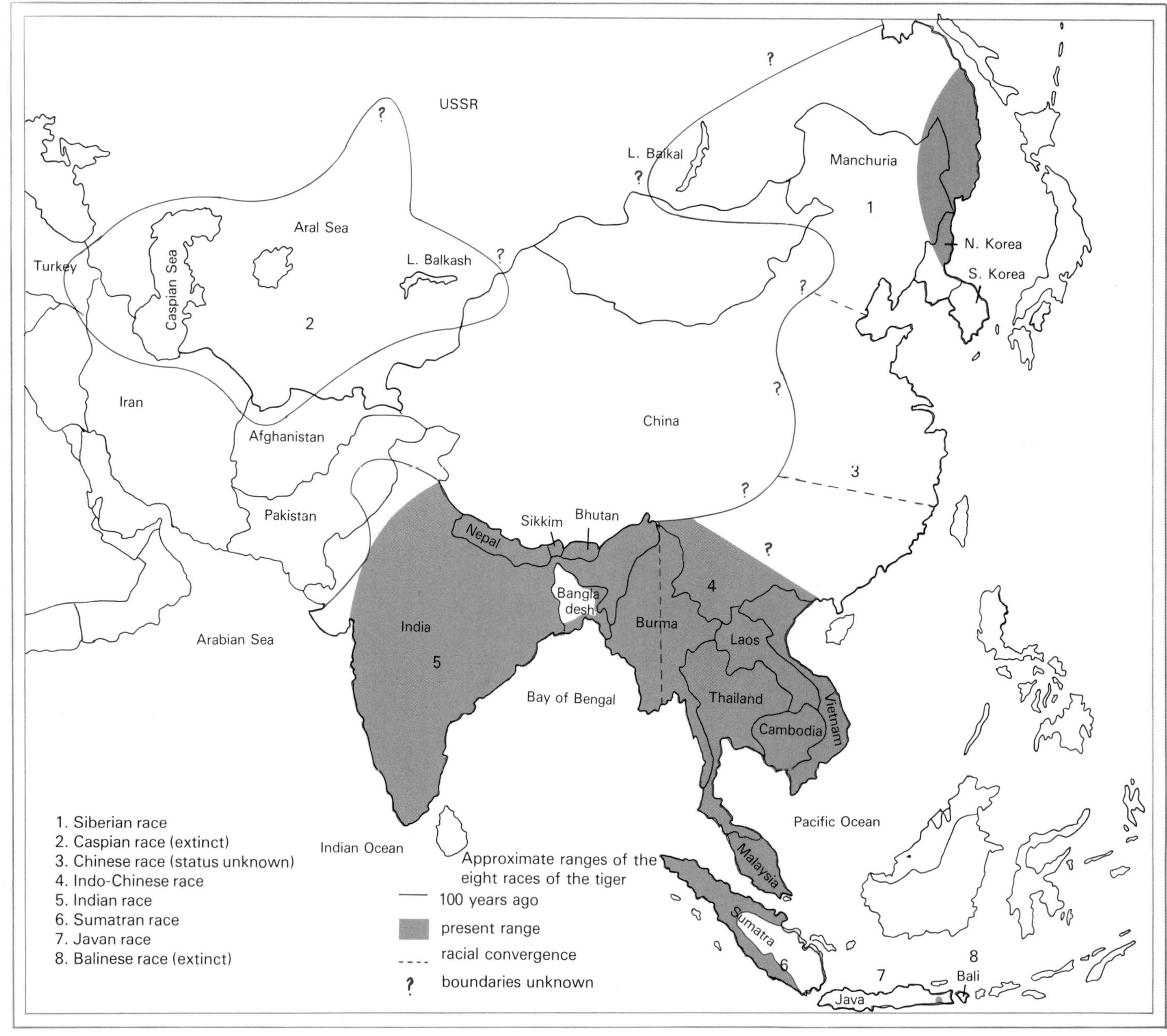

7. Map showing the distribution of tiger species.

grass thickets and in pine and fir forests to the south. In the USSR the Caspian race has adopted lowland reed-beds and montane cork-oak and tamarisk. Throughout the Indian subcontinent all types of forest seem acceptable, whether deciduous or evergreen, dry or humid and even thorn forests. In the Indian and Bangladeshi mangrove swamps of the Sunderbans and the mangrove areas of Sumatra it is completely at home in semi-aquatic surroundings. Along the southern slopes of the Himalayas tigers favour the rich forests of the lowland terai, but although they are seldom seen in the higher coniferous oak and rhododendron forests, they have not infrequently been recorded at altitudes of 12,000 feet and a few even at 13,000 feet. Throughout their huge range, indeed, the only limiting factors appear to be the availability of suitable prey, sufficient cover for hunting and ample sources of water, which are particularly vital to tigers in the hot south.

No two tigers have identical markings and the pattern of stripes varies considerably. The combination of bold black stripes on a golden-orange

8. Indian tiger in the snow. The Indian tiger has occasionally been recorded at altitudes as high as 13,000 feet in the Himalayas. The Siberian race can withstand temperatures as low as −30F.

background, with pure white on the face, belly and inner surfaces of the legs looks very conspicuous in a cage, but it provides a surprisingly perfect cryptic camouflage in the normal habitat. A motionless tiger standing in long, parched yellow grass almost dissolves from view, and even in the tangled vegetation of the green jungle, the alternation of black, orange and white merges astonishingly well into the pattern of broken sunlight and dense shadow. Several times while watching a motionless tiger, my attention has been momentarily distracted elsewhere and when I looked again it took me several minutes to re-locate the tiger, although it had not moved. Such camouflage is, of course, an essential element in the tiger's ability to stalk its prey unseen. The shape of the tiger's face towards its prey is wonderfully 'broken up' by the irregular black curves and spots around the cheeks and forehead, only the tawny nose being unmarked. The pattern of the bold black and white area above the eyes differs in each individual and provides, for tiger-watchers, a relatively simple means of identification.

9. (Left) *A splendid self-portrait of a tiger, obtained by setting a trip wire to trigger the camera flash.*

10 and 11. The tiger's colouration provides perfect camouflage, whether among dead leaves on the forest floor, as shown by the cub (right), *or resting in the long grass, like the watchful adult* (above).

12. Tiger swimming in the Delhi zoo.

The origin of the white tigers on show in zoos is particularly interesting. In 1951 a white male cub was trapped in the Rewa Forest in India and kept as a curiosity by the local maharajah. Later it was mated to a normally coloured tigress, which in time produced three normal litters from this sire. A female from the second litter was then mated to its father, the white tiger, and in 1958 it gave birth to four white cubs. The delighted Maharajah of Rewa turned over his disused summer palace at Govindgarh to the tigers. Later litters produced two more white males and a normal female and then a white pair. The Indian government agreed to share the cost of looking after them and declared them to be national treasures. Since then further white offspring have been sold to foreign zoos. The original sire is now dead, but white tigers still occupy the palace. They are not albinos (which would have pink eyes), but what scientists call 'recessive mutants'. Their stripes are dark

13. White tigers, seen in some zoos, are not albinos but descendants from a unique recessive mutant captured in India.

14. Many zoos fail to realize the importance of ample swimming facilities for tigers, which greatly enjoy playing in water.

brown on a whitish background and they have bluish eyes. There is only one record of a true albino tiger having been shot in India, but many pale or cream-coloured tigers have been killed.

Unlike lions, which are social animals living in family 'prides' of up to thirty individuals, tigers are solitary, the sexes meeting only briefly for mating. They are also chiefly, although not exclusively, nocturnal, and spend most of the day resting in vegetation near a stream or pool, in which they frequently lie to escape heat and flies. They are enthusiastic bathers, sometimes leaping into a pool with a great splash and obvious enjoyment. They swim powerfully and I have found their pug-marks plainly visible

15–17. Three types of prey. The beautiful chital (or axis deer) (above) *and the sambur* (below) *are both favourite prey for tigers. Wild pigs* (centre) *are also frequently taken by tigers, but a large boar can kill a tiger with its formidable tusks.*

18. The heavily armoured Indian rhinoceros has no fear of tigers, but its calves are sometimes taken.

on an island in the Bay of Bengal nearly five miles from the mainland.

The tiger is the dominant predator of Asia, firmly established at the apex of its ecological pyramid. It has an important role in helping to control the population of various animals such as deer and wild pigs. Significantly in regions where tigers have been exterminated in India, native villagers are now suffering heavy losses of crops from the inevitable population explosion of deer and pigs. Only now is the economic value of the tiger being recognized.

Food and methods of hunting

Although deer and pigs are the mainstay of the tiger's diet, it is catholic in its tastes and will eat a very wide variety of foods, from the one-ton gaur, or jungle bison, and occasionally young elephants or rhinoceroses of up to 1,000 pounds in weight, down to barking deer, hog deer and blackbuck, or even insignificant creatures such as crabs, turtles, fish, lizards, small birds, or locusts. Monkeys are frequently taken and in Malaysia the diminutive chevrotain, or mouse-deer, which is little larger than a rabbit, is much sought after. So also throughout its range is the big and powerful Indian porcupine, in spite of the fact that many tigers suffer injury or eventual death from the long spines which it drives into the face or lungs of its pursuer. As a change of diet tigers sometimes eat a variety of jungle fruits, including the football-size but evil-smelling durian, which is so much liked by the natives of Malaysia. Their stomachs often contain earth, although whether this is taken deliberately or perhaps inadvertently while eating a carcass is not clear. Normally most animal bones are eaten, but the contents of the rumen in the digestive tract of ungulates is invariably left. Contrary to the opinion of some writers, carrion is quite frequently eaten, including even unburied human corpses during the Vietnam war.

A tiger's appetite is almost incredible. As much as seventy pounds of meat

19. Indian porcupines are powerful animals weighing up to 40 pounds. Tigers frequently attack them and are injured or even eventually killed by the spines which are driven into their faces or chests when the porcupine suddenly backs into its pursuer.

20. Except for the largest prey, tigers usually prefer to straddle carcasses when they drag them, as this one is doing while crossing a dry stream bed.

21. A sub-adult tigress standing over the remains of its prey.

22. Tigers (including man-eaters) usually begin eating their prey at the rump, as shown by this picture of one with a domestic buffalo.

can be eaten in a single night from a large carcass, and in a couple of days there is often nothing left for the scavenging jackals and vultures, although these are usually quick to assemble around any kill.

On average a tiger kills large animals only once or twice a week and may go for quite long periods with little to sustain it but minor snacks. When it does succeed with large prey, however, it gorges to repletion.

A tiger will seldom eat large animals exactly where it has killed them. Usually the carcass is dragged to a suitable spot where the tiger is unlikely to be disturbed. At such moments one can appreciate its tremendous strength, which is concentrated in its massive shoulders and fore-legs. A full-grown sambur or barasingha stag weighing 500 pounds (as much as or more than the tiger's own weight) is dragged with little apparent effort; I have seen the carcass of a domestic buffalo cow dragged nearly 250 feet without pause.

23. It is unusual for a tiger to take a nap as close to the carcass of its prey as the one shown in this picture. It has just killed a buffalo.

24. The Barasingha or swamp deer is fairly rare, but it is also preyed upon by the tiger.

Schaller records finding the carcass of a chital deer which had been dragged for 1,800 feet. Even more remarkable was the occasion when he found that a tigress had *carried* the 142-pound forequarters of a cow for 600 feet along a stream bed and 100 feet up a mass of boulders without leaving any trace of drag marks. Another record tells of a tiger which killed a cow in a native compound and carried it away over a six-foot wall.

If the prey is not consumed at a single meal, the tiger hides the remains of the carcass by scraping earth and vegetation over it. The tiger then retires a short distance and lies out of sight while it digests its meal. However, the carcass is rarely hidden sufficiently to prevent vultures, jackals and other scavengers from finding it and the infuriated tiger sometimes rushes out to drive them away (plates 25–28).

25–28. A tiger notices some vultures eating its prey. It rushes towards them and hits out at one of them.

29. The ungainly nilgai are protected by the Hindus because of their resemblance to cows, but tigers prey upon them.

30. Having eaten part of a cow, a tiger drags the carcass, twice its own weight, to a safe hiding place.

31. Gaur, or jungle bison, inhabit hill forests. Bulls can weigh 2,000 pounds. Tigers normally prey upon cows and calves.

32. A tigress and cub feeding on a domestic buffalo.

33. Alert monkeys reveal the tiger's presence by chattering from the tree tops. Both the langur and the macaque are frequently killed by tigers on the ground.

34. Tigers are dependent on water not only for quenching their thirst but also for bathing. They often lie partially submerged to escape the flies.

With such power and skill as a hunter, the tiger might be thought likely to wipe out every other animal in the region. This is far from being so. Both Schaller and McDougal have shown that it fails to catch its prey far more often than it succeeds. Schaller suggested that there are nineteen unsuccessful attempts for a single success. One reason for this is that monkeys and peafowl frequently give vocal warning of the tiger's approach.

The tiger's method of hunting has now been extensively studied. It hunts by sight, the sense of smell being of very minor value. Both its eyesight and hearing are highly developed, however, as one would expect from an animal which normally hunts nocturnally in dense vegetation. Stories of tigers 'charging' after prey are largely illusory. It is essentially a stalking animal, which with great skill makes use of every scrap of cover in order to approach its prey unseen. It has infinite patience and will take fifteen or twenty minutes to creep over ground that it could cover at walking pace in a minute. Having approached to within fifty feet or less of its quarry, it will often wait to see whether the unsuspecting animal is likely to graze towards it and thus shorten the critical distance. If not, it rushes forward and seizes its prey. A large animal, such as a gaur, a buffalo, or a full-grown sambur stag, will usually be taken by the throat and held down until it dies of strangulation. Smaller animals may be killed by a single, powerful bite through the nape of the neck. In either case the neck vertebrae are usually severed by the tiger's long canines but, although death may be instantaneous, the tiger does not relax its grip for several minutes and will hold the neck of a large animal for as long as ten minutes to make sure that it has been strangled. Often the prey is bowled over at once by the sudden assault, but if in a split second it has seen the tiger emerging from cover it will turn to run, in which case the tiger may

35. Rocky outcrops and high ground are regularly used by tigers for watching the approach of prey, which is then stalked through the undergrowth.

36. Like tigers, leopards hunt chiefly at night but prey upon small animals, taking dogs and goats from around villages. Prey is often carried up a tree to be eaten.

be able only to seize its hindquarters. But the sheer weight and momentum of the attack are usually sufficient to bring the prey down and enable the tiger to transfer its bite to the throat or nape. If the prey is alert and agile enough to escape, the tiger seldom attempts to chase it, being much too heavy to run fast over any distance. Even animals which have been severely mauled by a tiger sometimes succeed in escaping, only to die later elsewhere.

Graphic descriptions of tigers making a tremendous leap on their prey are pure fantasy. All modern scientific observers are in agreement that, although the tiger rears up to reach the shoulders and neck of large prey, the hind feet stay on the ground. Young and inexperienced tigers often make a poor job of attacking large animals and merely succeed in biting a mouthful of flesh from the rump or a leg before their prey escapes.

Tigers are not completely invincible. Territorial fighting between

37. The Royal Chitwan Park at sunrise. It not only assures the future of the tiger in Nepal but protects a great variety of other wildlife and provides pleasure for tourists.

38. Packs of dholes, or wild dogs, sometimes kill a tiger, but only after losing half their numbers.

neighbouring tigers not infrequently ends in one of them being killed and sometimes also being eaten. Encounters with sloth bears and the more formidable Himalayan black bear may not always end in the tiger's favour, but leopards, which avoid tigers, are easily killed. Wild pigs, which are a major food source, occasionally succeed in killing a full grown tiger by slashing open its belly with their powerful tusks. Packs of dholes (wild dogs) are also known to have killed tigers, although only after losing half their numbers during the tiger's savage defence. A large number of tigers also eventually die as a result of pursuing porcupines, judging by the number of reports of them being shot or found dead with quills embedded in their lungs, faces and legs. Adult elephants, Indian rhinoceroses and crocodiles have been credited with killing an occasional tiger and when I was in the Chittagong Hill Tracts I heard of a gaur bull which succeeded, when attacked, in fatally goring and kneeling on a tiger. Such incidents, however, are rare and very few tigers in the prime of life are ever killed except by man.

Territory and the telemetry project

On reaching maturity tigers establish hunting territories, which they patrol regularly, sometimes covering twenty miles in a single night if no kill is made. The trails they use through the forest become well worn in time and their pug-marks are easily discernible in muddy or sandy areas. For ease of movement, they frequently use footpaths or roads created by foresters or villagers. High ground, ridges and rocky outcrops are favoured for the extra visibility they provide and the favourite grazing and wallowing or drinking places of deer are included in the circuit.

39–43. The Tiger Ecology Project team erect a cloth corridor into which a tiger will be driven (above left). *Dr Dave Smith awaits the tiger with a gun firing a tranquillizing syringe-dart. After being dart-gunned, the tiger walks a few hundred yards before losing consciousness. It is kept cool with water and fanning while being weighed and measured and is given any medical treatment required for injuries or sickness. Its feet are compared with pug-mark records; then a plastic collar with a miniature radio is fitted. The scientists then withdraw. The tiger regains consciousness and walks away, apparently unconcerned.*

Until the advent of the Nepal Tiger Ecology Project, little was known of the territorial activities of tigers because of the extreme difficulty of tracing their whereabouts at night, when they are most active. As part of 'Operation Tiger' (see pages 101–120), the Smithsonian Institution set up the Project with funds provided by the World Wildlife Fund to make a long-term study of the behaviour and social organization of tigers. Particular attention was given to their movements within their hunting areas. These were ascertained by the use of radio-telemetry, a technique that had been employed successfully for many years in research programmes in African and American wildlife reserves, although it had not yet been attempted either in Asia or with tigers. The work was undertaken in close collaboration with the Nepalese Government Office of National Parks and Wildlife Conservation. Two Nepalese, Mr Kirti Man Tamang and Mr Himanta Mishra, were important members of the team, which was led by Dr John C. Seidensticker. Others taking part were Dr Melvyn Sunquist, Dr J. L. D. Smith, Dale Miquelle and Dr Charles McDougal.

The site of the project was the Royal Chitwan National Park, an outstandingly beautiful reserve of 210 square miles (later enlarged to 500 square miles) in the undisturbed Rapti Valley of the terai between the foothills of the Himalayas and the Gangetic plain. The Park, which was relatively free from poaching thanks to an efficient guard-force, at that time contained about fifteen adult tigers and an equal number of sub-adults and young.

Today there are thirty adults in the park and twenty in the surrounding area. The dominant ungulates were the sambur and chital deer, although other species of deer and also many Indian rhinoceroses were present.

The radio-telemetry project involved temporarily immobilizing tigers with a dart-gun, the dart-syringe containing a carefully calculated dose of the drug 'CI-744', an immobilizing agent specially developed for cats. The animal to be darted was slowly driven by four elephants into a prepared area, on either side of which a strip of muslin had been erected on stakes, to form a gradual 'funnel' leading past trees in which two marksmen were hidden. When it was within 30 to 40 feet, one of the guns was fired, the dart hitting the tiger in the large muscle of the rump or shoulder. The prick of the syringe did not alarm the tiger unduly and it usually walked a further 300–500 yards before lying down and losing consciousness, its eyes remaining open. Five or six hours might pass before the drug wore off completely. During this time the tiger was carried in a sling to a shady spot, where it was kept cool by splashing with water and fanning. It was examined, given medical attention needed for any injury or sickness diagnosed, weighed, measured and photographed for identification. It was then fitted with a miniature radio transmitter embedded in a plastic collar. Each transmitter carried by a tiger emitted a 'bleep' signal on a different frequency, so that it could be monitored. Signals could be picked up at a distance of 200 to 3,000 yards, depending on the density of the intervening vegetation, by a receiver carried on an elephant. From a patrolling light aircraft the distance was increased to a maximum of twenty-five miles. When the tiger began to regain consciousness the scientists withdrew, leaving one member in concealment to make sure that it had suffered no after-effects and was able to walk away quite normally. On many occasions it was found later in the day at a fresh carcass.

In the course of six years, twenty-six tigers and six leopards were given radio collars, only one of which, a tigress in poor condition as a result of previous wounds and bone fractures, failed to recover from the drug; this was before the importance of preventing a rise in body temperature had been fully appreciated. With any endangered species such as the tiger the loss of a single animal in the course of research is regarded as a serious matter and precautions were immediately redoubled.

Although a collar may impair the natural dignity and beauty of the tiger, it is only by marking the individual in some way to distinguish it from its neighbours and to enable it to be monitored that any knowledge of its life-style, in particular its movements and interaction with others of its kind, can be gained. The radio collars do not appear to inconvenience the tigers in the least, and sentimental objections must surely be outweighed by the scientific benefits and the valuable information that is being built up.

The Chitwan Project revealed for the first time that male tigers held hunting territories as large as fifty square miles; that the territories of tigresses, which were usually contained within or overlapped those of males,

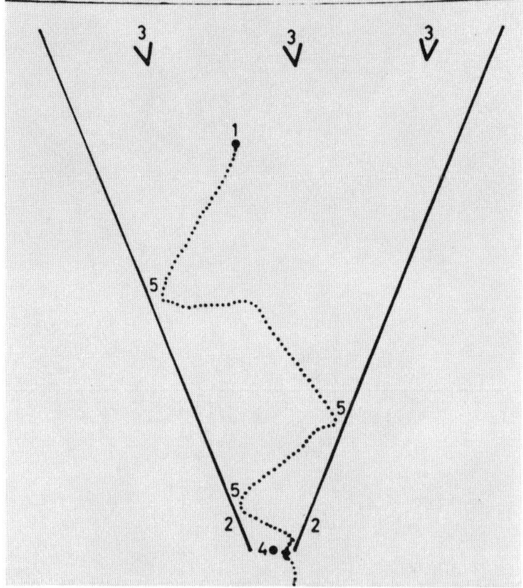

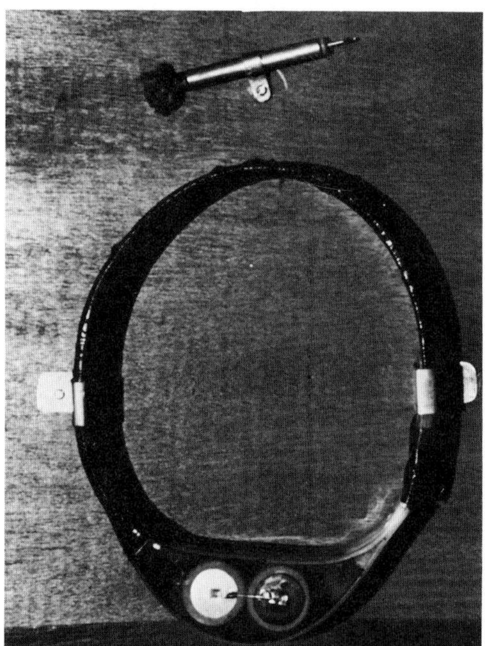

44. (Above) *A diagram showing how the tiger is dart-gunned. In the early morning hours a tiger is normally in the vicinity of a bait it had killed the night before (1). From a suitable location the beaters unfold and stretch the two continuous white sheets, the beat-*

cloths (2), each of which is about 600 yards long. Three or four elephants (3), their drivers hollering, then move down towards the neck of the funnel. Meanwhile a marksman is perched in a tree at the exit (4). The tiger retreats, turning away from the beat-cloth (5). It is finally darted from twenty yards or less to ensure that the projectile hits muscle tissue.

45. (Left) *The dart from a dart gun and a radio collar. The dart is fired from a modified shotgun. The impact triggers a charge inside the dart which drives the plunger forward and thus injects the drug. The collar weighs about 600 grams and causes the animal no discomfort. Lithium batteries run the transmitter for five years, but the plastic collar normally wears out after three or four.*

46. (Above) *Dr John Seidensticker removing the thorns from the paw of a sedated tiger.*

47. (Right) *The highest tree in the region had steps cut in it to enable those taking part in the 'Tiger Ecology Project' to carry the antenna aloft quickly when tracking a radio-collared tiger.*

48. Tigers being monitored from an elephant.

were only a quarter to half as large; that territorial boundaries were by no means constant and usually contracted during the monsoon period; and that neighbouring tigers avoided conflict by keeping at least a mile or two from each other. The explorations of sub-adults of both sexes in search of territories were also plotted. It also became clear that whereas the territories of adult tigresses were held primarily to obtain food and protect the cubs, males were much more concerned with containing and mating with as many females in condition to breed as possible. The studies are continuing and are gradually building a mass of information which will be of immense value in the management of other tiger reserves throughout Asia.

49. (Above) *Trackers coming across a tiger that has been dart-gunned.*

50. *From a Landrover or elephant the movements of a collared tiger can be plotted from a distance of two to three miles. From a light plane the distance is increased to about 25 miles.*

Conclusions reached in the Chitwan research cannot, of course, be taken as necessarily representative of other regions of Asia, where many factors are different. The sizes of territories vary according to the density of the tiger population, the abundance of prey and the type of habitat. For example, studies by the Russian scientist Novikov show that the Siberian tigers have winter territories as large as 187 to 250 square miles in the cold taiga forests of Manchuria, where the chief prey species are pig, moose, wapiti and roe, musk and sika deer. In some of the smaller Indian tiger reserves, territories must be uncomfortably restricted by comparison even with Chitwan.

A remarkable and essential member of the Smithsonian team at Chitwan was Prem Badahur Rai. His father and grandfather had been chief shikaris to the Kings of Nepal and he had inherited their skills in tracking tigers and other animals to a degree which bordered on the miraculous. I had the pleasure of his company during a recent visit to Chitwan, where he told me

51. (Left) *A tiger rubbing a tree which a tigress has sprayed.*

52. (Above) *Tigers sharpen their claws on favourite trees, raking the bark to a depth of half an inch. Such trees often become territorial markers.*

53. (Above right) *The famous tracker Prem Badahur Rai with a tiger's skull. He plays an important part in the 'Tiger Ecology Project'.*

54. (Right) *Measuring the height to which a tiger has reached when sharpening its claws. In this unusual example the height was 9 feet* $10\frac{1}{2}$ *inches, reached by springing at the trunk.*

the story of his attempt to save four twelve-week-old tiger cubs whose mother had been killed. Orphaned cubs of this age have no chance of survival unless taken to a zoo, but Prem does not like zoos and believed he could accomplish something never before attempted – raising the cubs in the wild. Knowing their extreme vulnerability, yet neither wishing to bring them into captivity nor habituate them to hand-feeding, he faced an almost impossible task. First he erected a large enclosure around the area where they lay hidden, using the white cotton sheeting employed by the Smithsonian team in constructing the 'funnel' into which tigers are driven when being dart-gunned. Four big lamps were erected in trees at the corners, which at least deterred predators from finding the cubs. Fresh meat was scattered inside the enclosure for the cubs. Unfortunately, they soon broke out and disappeared. Prem scattered sand on the surrounding trails and a few days later found their pug-marks. By dragging fresh meat to lay scent trails he gradually lured them back into the enclosure. One cub disappeared, but the others readily took the meat which Prem kept supplying and they remained in comparative security behind the flimsy walling. As the weeks passed, new problems arose. At different times no fewer than seven adult tigers were attracted by the smell of fresh meat and Prem repeatedly had to drive them off while keeping watch on the enclosure. The cubs had by now doubled in size and were thriving. Two months later they broke out and began moving towards the forested Churia Hills on the boundary of the park. Prem patiently followed their tracks, leaving meat for them at intervals. Finally, to his delight, he found they had killed a young chital deer, although having only milk teeth (which they retain for a year) they had not succeeded in breaking the skin and eating it. Hidden in a tree, he watched them returning to the kill and on the third night had the satisfaction of seeing them tear open the carcass and eat it. For four long months he had devoted all his time to the cubs, which now appeared to have a reasonable chance of survival providing they avoided contact with a territory-holding adult of their kind. I found his story, so modestly told in hesitant English, singularly moving. The later history of the cubs is not known.

Scent as a biochemical 'finger-print'

Like domestic cats, tigers mark their territories by squirting a pungent scent on foliage or rocks along their established trails. They also leave their dung and scrapes in conspicuous places. Favourite trees are used regularly for sharpening their claws and these well-marked trunks, which are powerfully raked to a height of six or seven feet, may also act as territorial signposts intended to prevent conflict with trespassers.

Tigers of both sexes make a curious grimace when smelling the powerful odour of the secretions which they spray on foliage (see plate 56). In this so-called *flehmen* response the nose and lips are strongly wrinkled and the tongue lolls out of the open mouth. The bulk of the liquid is urine, but it also contains a whitish secretion from a gland near the anus, and it is this that provides the distinctive odour, which can even be detected by a human nose

55. (Left) *An Indo-Chinese tiger spraying scent. Territorial scent marking is an important function in social organization.*

56. *A typical grimace of a tiger smelling its own scent, with the mouth open and tongue hanging out.*

for many days after it has been secreted. The substance, called a pheromone, has recently been analysed by a distinguished Indian scientist, Dr R. L. Brahmachary of the Indian Statistical Institute in Calcutta, working in collaboration with Dr. J. Dutta of the Bose Research Institute. By means of chromatography and other laboratory analysis a distinctive amine, peculiar to the tiger, was discovered. Various experiments with four captive tigers established that this amine, together with hormones and other substances, not only identified the species, but also served to communicate the sex and sexual condition; moreover, that it also serves as a 'biochemical fingerprint', the secretion of each tiger being slightly different. This important discovery throws an entirely new light on the value of territorial marking as a means whereby neighbouring tigers can identify each other as individuals and also know if tigresses in the area are coming into condition for mating. It was hoped that the different races of tigers might be distinguished by this analysis, but work in the laboratory of the Zoological Society of London suggests that this is not so. The study of pheromones is still in its infancy, although their importance as a sexual attractant or behaviour regulator in insects (such as the queen-bee substance which inhibits the development of unwanted queens) has long been known.

Territorial marking, then, serves several purposes. It advertises the presence of the holder of the territory and warns potential male trespassers to stay out, thus minimizing actual conflict which would be harmful to survival. Without this form of advertisement a male tiger could not hold so large a territory effectively. Marking is also a kind of intelligence service, enabling tigers to know which individuals of their kind have passed by. Finally it serves the important function of enabling the resident male to locate tigresses the moment they come into oestrus and are ready to mate. Wandering adults, sub-adults and young tigers do, of course, enter the established territories of other tigers, but scent-marking regulates their presence.

Vocalization

Tigers are not very vocal animals, although territorial encounters or squabbles over a kill can occasionally be both noisy and protracted. Vocalization takes several forms and has been painstakingly analysed by

57. John Aspinall has bred many tigers under ideal conditions on his estate near Canterbury. They have developed a remarkable rapport with him.

58. When the tiger roars, its ears are laid back, the eyes narrow, and the nose wrinkles.

Schaller and McDougal. The big cats of the genus *Panthera* such as lions and tigers roar, whereas the smaller cats of the genus *Felidae* such as the lynx, jungle cat and desert cat, make only mewing, coughing or snarling sounds. The roar of a wild tiger is a sound which, once heard, is unlikely to be forgotten, particularly if heard, as I first heard it, in the dead of night. It is, however, surprisingly infrequent and seems to be employed only when challenging other tigers at long range, or when searching for contact with the opposite sex. The most commonly heard sound is a deep growl, which at high intensity turns into a shorter, cough-like noise and at low intensity into a snarling sound. McDougal differentiates the two, believing that the growl is probably aggressive and the snarl defensive, which may well be true. The snarl can also turn into a hissing, spitting sound very similar to, although much louder than, that made by a domestic cat. Then there is the long moaning sound, which obviously lacks emotional intensity and seems to serve chiefly as a means of passive communication, although it may sometimes precede a roar. Tigresses use it to keep in touch with young cubs in dense vegetation.

A variety of minor vocalizations occur, such as grunting, woofing and purring and the so-called 'pooking', which writers have described as resembling the alarm call of a sambur deer. Finally there is the curious puffing sound made through the nose, which I would write as 'prrru'. I first heard this when John Aspinall was showing me his tigers at Howletts in Kent. His animals are superbly housed, with large paddocks which include big trees and swimming pools. They have become so tame and contented that John is able to take them for walks in the park and to romp with them. During one such romping session two tigers on different occasions rubbed their cheeks against

his thigh and made the puffing sound. Later, when they had returned to their enclosure, one of them rubbed its cheek against the bars and when I fondled its ear it immediately repeated the sound, which I suspect denotes pleasure.

Reproduction

The tiger mates promiscuously with any tigress it can find in oestrus condition within reach of its territory. In the Nepalese tiger project one male was known to have mated with five different females which lived in or entered its territory and to have associated with no fewer than nine others. (It is interesting to note that only with the ability to identify individual animals accurately could the research team have ascertained this.) The tigress advertises her condition by the scent which she leaves at frequent intervals on vegetation or rocks and by occasional roaring or moaning. Males quickly respond and gravitate towards her, but although she is usually willing to be served by any one of them, the holder of the territory, being familiar with her movements, normally gets there first. Initially she may react aggressively towards him and until copulation takes place there is usually little actual contact between the pair. The male first has to subdue the female's initial aggressive reaction, which if she is not ready to mate can be fierce. The male does this by approaching cautiously and lying down passively, first in one place then another. After a while the tigress may copy this procedure and they gradually draw nearer to each other. This sequence, with many withdrawals and tentative advances, eventually leads to more obvious courtship play, which may include cautious pawing, flank and cheek rubbing, licking, quiet moaning or grunting and nasal puffing. McDougal, who is one of the few to have watched a protracted courtship in detail, saw a tigress actually roll herself right over the recumbent male and

59–61. The courtship of tigers is not always successful because of the initially aggressive reaction of the tigress (left). *If she is ready to copulate, the tiger seizes her by the nape of the neck, often lacerating her.*

take his great head between her paws as a demonstration of submission.

Copulation in zoo tigers is a fairly straightforward affair with a relatively high rate of success. In the wild it is often both rough and noisy, probably because of the much shorter time the male has for breaking down the female's ambivalent aggression. Unsuccessful mating is frequent. During copulation, the male grasps the female with his teeth by the back of her neck, which is often lacerated. When he dismounts she may attempt a vicious swipe at him. At the climax the male frequently moans or roars. As the female cannot ovulate until impregnated, copulation is repeated many times and may be continued at intervals for as long as two days. McDougal mentions that an American zoo recorded that a pair of captive tigers copulated 106 times in four days, a record among the big cats beaten only by a lion in Africa, observed by George Schaller, which achieved 157 copulations in 57 hours. Occasionally a pair of mated tigers maintain a social contact even after the tigress has passed the seven-day oestrus period, but this is unusual. Normally they soon go their own way and may not see each other again until the tigress is next ready to mate two years later if she rears her cubs successfully. Each will know of the other's presence, however, because of territorial marking. During the intervening period the tigress will not come into oestrus, although in zoos tigresses have been known to do so even while cubs were still being suckled. However, if the wild tigress loses her litter, or they are still-born, she may mate with the same male again, or with a different one, within five or six months.

After a gestation period of 14 to 15 weeks the cubs are born, blind and helpless, in a well hidden den. Litter sizes vary from one to an exceptional

seven cubs. In the artificial conditions of captivity, even in the most skilfully managed zoos, tigresses have a poor record for raising cubs, which often have to be taken from them to prevent them from being abandoned or even eaten. They are then bottle-fed, the keeper becoming their surrogate mother, and they are deprived of the care and comfort which they should receive from the tigress. Nevertheless many zoos have become very successful at rearing cubs in this manner, with the result that there is a surplus of captive tigers.

62 and 63. Litters of four are commonplace in zoos, but in the wild this litter would be unusually large. Captive tigresses often kill or abandon their cubs, but keepers have become expert in bottle-feeding them (right).

In the wild, conditions are very different. Both pre-natal and post-natal mortality are very high and the first year of a cub's life is fraught with many dangers. The tigress is alone, without a mate to help her. When a lioness has cubs, other lionesses (the 'aunts' in the pride) help to guard them. They kill game from which she can snatch a quick meal. When the tigress leaves the den, the cubs are at the mercy of every passing jackal, hyena, wild dog, leopard or python. If their sire or another vagrant tiger should come across the cubs, they may even make a casual meal of them. There are indeed records of cubs nearly a year old being killed by adult tigers.

Grass fires are another frequent hazard to young cubs. Between each monsoon season fires are started by villagers in order to improve the grazing for their wandering cattle, which compete with deer for the grass in the forest glades. Many tiger cubs are found burnt to death in or near their dens.

64. A litter of five cubs born in captivity to a tigress of the Indian race.

The cubs' eyes usually open during their second week of life and at this stage are pale blue-green, changing later to amber. Cubs do not leave the den until they are between four and eight weeks old and are not fully weaned until they reach the age of five or six months. The first few times they venture into the dangerous world outside the den are particularly critical. Staggering through the long grass, they move in single file behind the tigress, trying to keep her in sight. Her striped tail and the large white spot behind each ear probably serve as 'follow me' signals. During these first forays the last cub in the line, usually the weakest of the litter, is very vulnerable to being picked off by a predator. In large litters the runt rarely survives long enough to emerge, often being either smothered or starved.

The dice are heavily loaded against cubs, and it is rare for a wild tigress to raise more than two to maturity from a successful litter every second year. Both Schaller and McDougal have studied this problem statistically. They agree that in spite of her high reproductive potential, her devotion to her young and her ability to replace lost litters so quickly, the tigress is unlikely to improve on a lifetime average of raising one cub a year to maturity. According to zoo records the average size of zoo-born tiger litters is 2.8 (Schaller). Because the majority are hand-reared and carefully looked after, most of them reach maturity. The maximum longevity of zoo tigers is about

65 *and* 66. (Above and below left) *These charming pictures of a Sumatran tigress with her cubs were taken in Whipsnade Zoo, where the Zoological Society of London has established an excellent breeding record.*

67. (Above) *A zoo-bred Siberian tiger taking a rest on its mother's back.*

68 and 69. Mortality among cubs is high once they venture outside the carefully hidden den. When the tigress leaves to go hunting, every passing predator, including their own sire, is likely to kill them.

70. Two tiger cubs going exploring.

twenty years and the record number of young produced by a captive tigress is thirty. Assuming that free-living tigresses live as long as eighteen years, Schaller calculates that, if a tigress produces her first litter in her fourth year, her theoretical total lifetime production will be about fourteen. But, as he points out, the pressure on tigers throughout Asia is so heavy that it is doubtful whether the average tigress lives this long or can raise even half this number. This poor rate of replacement has been one of the factors in the decline of the tiger.

Education of the cubs

Cubs grow quickly and in their rough-and-tumble games soon begin to learn the skills they will require for hunting and survival. At first the tigress hides them in the undergrowth when she goes hunting. As they grow larger and

71. A tigress and cub.

more self-reliant she allows them to watch her and finally to join the hunt. Soon the half-grown cubs attack the prey with her but, because of their eagerness and inexperience, often let it escape. Initially they go for the legs of the prey, which if it happens to be a large stag or a wild pig is able to retaliate with antlers or tusks. Cubs are often gored or killed and some have been trampled to death when unwisely attacking a herd of buffaloes. The tigress usually intervenes, but apparently also occasionally permits the cubs to make fools of themselves, as part of the training process (see plate 72). Nearly two years pass before the cubs have fully learnt, by watching the tigress, that they must go immediately for the throat or the nape-bite and how to topple large animals off their feet. Once they have mastered this, the family breaks up and the now full-grown cubs disperse to establish their own territories. They will not reach sexual maturity for another year, however.

72. A young tiger inexpertly attacks the legs of a buffalo. The tigress pulls it down by the rump before killing it with the usual throat bite.

This long but essential tutelage cannot, of course, be duplicated in zoos. It has become customary, in recent years, for zoos and 'safari parks' to respond to the growing public interest in conservation by claiming that by keeping endangered animals such as the tiger in captivity they are ensuring the survival of the species. Some officials have even maintained that the intention is to return surplus tigers to the wild. Although many famous zoos, by establishing gene-banks of endangered species, are undoubtedly making a major contribution to conservation, such talk shows an astonishing ignorance of the free-born tiger. Not having been taught from birth to maturity the skills of hunting, such tigers would either die of starvation, be killed by the first wild tiger they met, or be obliged to take very easy prey such as domestic animals and humans and would therefore be quickly shot. Moreover, although zoo-bred tigers are usually well cared for, they are

73. A tigress with two cubs who are sleeping, well-hidden, in the background.

deprived of everything they need and enjoy in the wild except plentiful food. They may be healthy and contented in captivity, but in-breeding and the lack of mental and physical stimulus result in progressive cerebral degeneration which would make it almost impossible for them to adapt to the hazards of life in the jungle. Returning social animals such as ungulates and even lions to the wild is possible, but for the solitary tiger, which depends for survival on a two-year tutelage by its mother, this is virtually impossible.

Man-eating by tigers

To round off the biography of the tiger there remains the question of the habitual man-eater – the favourite theme of the tiger-hunter. Man-killing and man-eating are exceptional aspects of the behaviour of the species. Far from habitually attacking humans, tigers prefer to give them a wide berth. If

74. The victim of a tiger surrounded by villagers. The tiger had an injured shoulder.

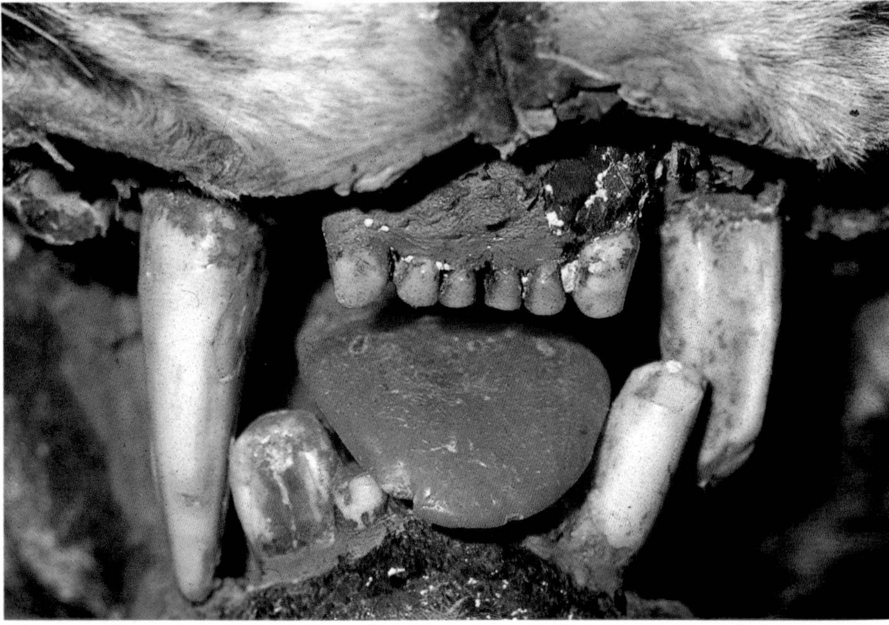

75. The jaws of a man-eater. Man-eating is usually the result of inability to hunt normal prey because of injury or loss of teeth as in this example.

they meet them they almost always turn away, either immediately or after a brief inspection. There is evidence from artifacts that man has hunted tigers for five thousand years; certainly ever since the invention of the spear tigers have had good reason to learn to avoid him. For the last hundred years his approach has almost invariably meant death or maiming. Only in the last few years have tigers, in a very few long-established reserves such as the Kanha and the Chitwan, begun to regard man as anything but a fearsome enemy.

How, then, should we view the undoubted fact that some tigers do seek out, kill and eat humans? How often does this happen? And why?

There are authentic accounts from the time of the great tiger-hunters of rogue tigers terrifying whole groups of villages. In 1856, for example, more than 200 villagers were killed by tigers in one district of Mandla in the Central Provinces. Stuart Baker, writing in 1890, described how a tiger 'took

76. A splendid portrait of a tiger growling.

77. Two young tigers showing no fear of the photographer, Charles McDougal, who has studied tigers in Nepal for many years.

possession of the road and actually stopped the traffic. It was a merciless highwayman, which levied toll upon the drivers of native carts, not only by an attack on their bullocks, but by seizing the driver himself.' In 1902 the Indian government recorded a total of 1,046 people as having been killed by tigers in that year. Even today, when tigers are so scarce in India, they still kill forty or more people a year out of a population of about 625 millions. To put these figures in perspective, however, one has to remember that at least one hundred people die from snake bites in India for each one killed by a tiger. Deaths by traffic accidents on India's overcrowded and undisciplined highways are infinitely more numerous.

Not surprisingly, deaths caused by tigers are always reported in the press, whereas those by snake-bite or road accidents are too commonplace to be regarded as newsworthy. The killing of humans by tigers cannot, of course, be ignored and the culprit is today immediately hunted and shot, usually by local officials and forest guards. Unfortunately other quite innocent tigers are also often killed on such occasions in mistake for the real culprit, or for the black market value of their skins.

It is now generally accepted that a tiger takes to killing humans either because it has been incapacitated by injury, wounds or the loss of teeth in old age, which prevent it from killing its normal prey, or because the local deer and pigs have been exterminated by farmers anxious to protect their crops. Once a tiger learns how easy it is to kill a man, it will probably do so again and may pass on the habit to other tigers. The eating of an unburied human corpse may also lead to the killing of live humans and this probably accounted for the reports of tigers preying on isolated sentries or wounded soldiers during the Korean and Vietnam wars.

Human deaths now occur chiefly among villagers who, having grown up in tiger country, have little fear of meeting them. Indeed, in some parts of India villagers are so accustomed to the presence of tigers that they refer to them by pet names and are quite philosophical about the occasional loss of a dog or a cow. Unfortunately they ignore the regulations which have been introduced for their protection and enter reserved forests or wildlife reserves to harvest grass or firewood. They also illegally create plantations of maize or sugar cane in protected areas and regularly allow their cattle to trespass in such places. The basic cause of death to humans today is the progressive disappearance of the tiger's habitat and prey, which inevitably increases the number of likely confrontations between a hungry tiger and a solitary villager. A sudden and serious outburst of man-eating by five tigers in Uttar Pradesh State in 1979, which was carefully investigated by Dr S.L. Choudhury, a Director of the Indian Tiger Project, undoubtedly had this origin.

Man-eating does not occur throughout the whole geographical range of the tiger. It has not been recorded anywhere in the region of the Siberian race for the past seventy years. Today the only region where it persists and has persisted since the eighteenth century is in the Sunderbans, a labyrinth of mangrove swamps and tidal waterways encompassing some 3,000 square

78. A family portrait. The tigress is on watch while her three cubs sleep.

79. A young tiger is surprised at close quarters.

80. A delightful picture of a tiger relaxing which raised a lot of money for 'Operation Tiger'.

miles of the delta of the Ganges and Brahmaputra, two-thirds of which are in Bangladesh and one-third in India. When a survey was made in 1971 it was discovered that there were about 300 tigers in the Bangladesh area and another 195 in the Indian part. This is the largest contiguous population of tigers anywhere in the subcontinent. When I led an expedition in 1967 to explore this fascinating area and to investigate the man-eaters, officials at Khulna produced records showing that 265 people had been killed by tigers in the past ten years in the Bangladesh area. The total for the Indian part was not recorded, but as the human population westward towards Calcutta is far greater than in the rest of the Sunderbans, the figure was thought to be probably even higher there.

Apart from the northern part of the Bangladeshi Sunderbans, where the tidal flooding penetrates only during typhoon periods, the region is largely uninhabited. I was therefore at a loss to know how such high casualties could occur. Once we entered the swamps, however, the reason became clear. Thousands of fishing boats and canoes ply between the mainland villages and the Bay of Bengal. Many of these carry wood-cutters who harvest timber and firewood from the sundri trees and golpatta palm leaves for thatching. Honey-collectors also land on the islands to take wild bees' nests, the combs and grubs of which are pulped to extract honey. It is very easy for tigers to stalk and kill a man engaged in these tasks among such a tangle of vegetation. Moreover, the semi-aquatic tigers do not hesitate to take men from canoes. I was told that one bold tiger swam out to a large Forest Department motor launch in broad daylight and had to be driven off with an oar.

81. (Left) *A flashlight picture of a tiger patrolling its territory at night.*

82. (Above) *A tiger bathing in a water tank, which was built to provide water for wildlife in droughts.*

The question remained: why were Sunderbans tigers man-eaters? A possible factor might be the scarcity of large prey animals, as the big barasingha, or swamp deer, had long since been exterminated by hunters; but there were still plenty of chital, or axis deer, and pigs.

After returning to England I discussed the problem with experts at the International Union for Conservation of Nature and Natural Resources,* who arranged for a German scientist, Dr Herbert Hendricks, to make a closer study. This included pathological examination of all tigers shot as man-eaters. The result, while not conclusive, was interesting. First Dr Hendricks pointed out that the scarcity of fresh water sources in the swamps forced the tigers to ingest a great deal of salt from the tidal rivers. This appeared to have damaged the livers and kidneys of the tigers examined. Whether this contributed to man-eating was perhaps a matter of conjecture. The most important discovery, made by mapping the localities where men were killed and comparing this with the distribution and behaviour of the tigers, was that only 3 per cent of the tigers attacked humans. The remainder reacted quite normally by avoiding them. Finally, all the tigers shot as man-eaters were either very emaciated, lame, had lost teeth, or had been previously wounded by shot-gun or rifle. This study is continuing in the new reserves which India and Bangladesh have now created for the protection of the Sunderbans tigers. Fresh-water tanks are also being erected for them.

Bearing in mind that the already dense human population of Asia will double in the next thirty years and that forests where tigers live will continue to disappear, one can forecast that the problem of man-eating will in the long term probably be solved the hard way. Tigers will eventually disappear except in the well-managed national parks and wildlife reserves, in which their natural prey will be maintained at a plentiful level.

*Usually referred to as the I.U.C.N., this is the leading scientific and non-governmental organization concerned with the conservation of the world's living natural resources; it works in close association with the World Wildlife Fund (W.W.F.) at their joint headquarters in Gland, Switzerland.

The Downfall of the Tiger

There is not the least doubt that tigers were once extremely numerous in Asia. In fact as late as the beginning of the last century they were still so plentiful in some parts of India that, as Brader wrote, 'it was a question whether man or the tiger would survive.'

Countless seals, figurines, vases, tiles, temple ornaments and paintings from the early civilizations in Asia depict tigers. Even before the Indo-Aryans arrived in the Indus Valley, the Harappa civilization of the Bronze Age was using the image of a tiger on its seals. The first Moghuls and the early Chinese and Indonesian rulers also revered tigers. The Pharaohs and Romans imported them for gladiatorial contests or as a public spectacle. Tiger-hunting became the sport of kings and remained so for several thousand years.

Hunting tigers with spears or bows and arrows, on foot, or horseback, or on elephants, left the odds in favour of the tiger and made no impression on its numbers. It was not until the advent of the matchlock gun in the fifteenth century that they could be killed at a safer distance; even then the first smooth-bore weapons were so inaccurate and lacking in power that the odds changed little. However, with the development of the rifled barrel, the flint-lock and more powerful bullets in the seventeenth century, the situation altered. With such weapons the odds were heavily and permanently against the tiger. Today a modern big-game rifle with a telescopic sight can fire an expanding bullet with a striking power of 5,000 pound/feet, or $2\frac{1}{2}$-ton shock-force, which, if aimed sufficiently accurately, can kill a tiger at a distance of half a mile.

At the time of the British Raj in India, tiger-hunting was the favourite pastime of Army officers and senior civil servants. The numerous Indian princes and rulers were only too happy to organize elaborate hunts for them which became great social occasions attended by hundreds of beaters and

83. A tiger growling at the photographer as it rests after a meal. It is missing a canine tooth.

servants. The British brought with them their strict code of sportsmanship and were scrupulous in insisting on following and dispatching any wounded animal. The game laws which they introduced, and particularly the division of forests into 'reserved blocks' were the first hesitant steps towards a conservation policy, although scarcely recognized as such at the time. 'Reserved' was more concerned with hunting than with forestry or the preservation of wildlife.

84 and 85. Large retinues of servants used to be employed during tiger hunts. (Above) *The trophy is carried back to camp.* (Below) *From comfortable chairs the hunters watch it being skinned.*

Methods of tiger-hunting varied. The adventurous would go into the forest with a congenial companion, a tracker and a couple of gun-bearers and camp in an area where they might bag a tiger or two. Organized hunts were on a much larger scale. Tigers were sometimes rounded up by beaters and driven like partridges to the waiting guns. Sportsmen were comfortably seated in elephant *howdahs*, in concealed *machans* (tree hides), or in the safety of *agots* (strongly constructed and fully enclosed hides at ground level). On more modest occasions tethered buffaloes were usually staked out near *machans* or *agots* to bring tigers within close range.

In Nepal a more lethal method of hunting was popular. When the King entertained important guests, two or three hundred elephants surrounded an area where tigers were numerous and gradually drove them to the centre. When the ring was closed, a wall of cotton fabric was erected from elephant to elephant to deter them from attempting to break out. The slaughter then began as the tigers emerged from the long grass. By this method bags were often very large. For example, at a hunt in 1919, 120 tigers, 27 leopards and 15 sloth bears were killed. One of the last ceremonial hunts of this kind attended by British royalty was in 1911, when King George V and his party shot thirty-nine tigers in eleven days. Times have changed: when the late Prince William of Gloucester was invited to a similar spectacle a few years ago, he politely replied that he would much rather be given the opportunity to photograph a Nepalese tiger.

Losses caused by hunting

Many British hunters of the past century succeeded in killing more than a hundred tigers. Rice, for example, claimed to have shot 158 in Rajasthan in four years, and Colonel Nightingale shot more than 300 in the Hyderabad region. Such figures were dwarfed, however, by those of the Indian maharajahs. The Maharajah of Udaipur shot at least 1,000 tigers and in 1965 the elderly Maharajah of Surguja informed George Schaller that his total was 'one thousand and fifty only.' Most Indian princes bagged their first tiger when they were ten to twelve years old and continued hunting until too old to carry a gun, whereas most of the British were in India on limited periods of duty.

Almost without exception these latter-day tiger hunters have become conservation-minded. It is a fascinating experience to talk to an octogenarian retired general or colonel of the Indian Army and to hear first-hand of the days when tigers could be seen and shot in places now overrun by the bustling cities of the subcontinent. Some of the most famous tiger-hunters

86. Tiger hunting by Prince Umed Singh of Kotah is portrayed in this early Nepalese picture. The tigers are being beaten into a bamboo enclosure where the hunters can easily shoot them.

87 and 88. At the turn of the century it was difficult without offending the hospitable Indian maharajahs to escape the social obligation to shoot tigers. (Left) *Lord Curzon, Governor General (1899–1905), with his tiger.* (Above) *One of the Maharajah of Bhopal's elephants with another victim.*

89. In some parts of Asia it is believed that the courage of a tiger is gained by eating its flesh. This photograph shows Cambodians picking at the flesh on a tiger skeleton.

were also excellent naturalists, who took a real interest in all forms of wildlife. The greatest of these was undoubtedly Jim Corbett, whose *Man-eaters of Kumaon* is one of the best books ever written about tigers. He was one of the first people to express concern at the decline in the tiger population and to prophesy that under the pressure of hunting and the growing exploitation of Indian forests the species was heading towards ultimate extinction. Such was his renown in India that he became the first and only Englishman to have a national park named after him. The beautiful Corbett National Park, in the Siwalik foothills of Uttar Pradesh, although now partly spoiled by a hydro-electric development which has flooded its lowlands, is still well known for its tigers.

The abjectly poor villagers of the Asian forests very rarely possessed firearms until well after the First World War, when a few headmen were allowed ancient shotguns to protect their crops from pigs and deer. Occasionally they might succeed in shooting a tiger, but usually only wounded it with pellets. Nevertheless, they did kill tigers with fall-traps or poison, chiefly in order to protect their cattle or children. In some parts of Asia, however, notably in China, Indo-China and Burma, tigers were and still are killed because of the belief that by eating their raw flesh the hunters gain the tiger's courage. In Taiwan 'wine' made from tiger bones procured in Thailand and Sumatra is still offered for sale. A wide variety of traps is used, the most common being a carefully camouflaged pit lined with bamboo spears, or spears fixed on a heavy log suspended over a tiger trail and released by a trip-wire. For both these a pig is usually tethered nearby. Either method is, of course, equally lethal to a passing human.

The use of poison for killing tigers is a rather more recent development. At first poisons from various plants were used. But when the United Nations began sending pesticides and crop sprays to aid agriculture, the farmers were quick to learn that if these poisons were liberally sprinkled on a carcass they would kill tigers and leopards. Moreover they would provide a useful source of income from the sale of skins unblemished by bullet-holes. Unfortunately the poisoned carcasses also killed huge numbers of useful scavengers such as vultures and jackals, to the detriment of the health of the villagers.

After the Second World War, the partition of India and the subsequent wars throughout south-east Asia, thousands of army rifles and automatic weapons found their way into the hands of villagers and nomadic tribes,

90. A pregnant tigress caught by the toes in a poacher's trap. After World War II, the hunting, trapping and poisoning of tigers reached catastrophic proportions. Shooting was becoming excessive during the last days of the British Raj, one maharajah shooting 1,150 tigers.

from Afghanistan to Korea. Efforts to reclaim them were largely unsuccessful. In the general decline of law and order, with rapidly changing forms of government, villagers believed it to be their democratic right to go where they wished and to hunt as they pleased. Poor and rich alike could now shoot tigers and sell their skins. The decline in tiger populations became even more rapid.

Two major political decisions were responsible for virtually wiping out the Caspian and Chinese races of the tiger. The Russian and Chinese governments embarked on massive land reclamation programmes in order to increase agricultural output. The Russian army was sent ahead of the farmers to exterminate the tigers in the area around the Caspian Sea, which they did very thoroughly. By the time this operation was completed, not only the tiger but the magnificent Caspian forests and the vast reed thickets of the littoral, where the tigers lived, had been cleared to make way for rice, tea and cotton crops. In China a government proclamation required all tigers to be exterminated as 'harmful to agricultural and pastoral progress'. It can be assumed that this order was also faithfully executed.

As tigers became increasingly scarce in the Indian subcontinent, hunters from all over the world hurried there to bag trophies before it was too late. Shikar outfitters did a roaring trade with wealthy Americans, Japanese, Germans and oil-rich sheikhs from the Persian Gulf. Simultaneously the prices of tiger-skin rugs and coats soared to record levels. On New York's Fifth Avenue such coats were soon selling at $4,000. By then India had introduced a partial ban on hunting, but there was a thriving black market and Customs officials and ship and aircraft crews were bribed to smuggle

91. Although tigers are now protected, there is still a market in their skins, as in this Peking shop.

skins. Throughout the subcontinent and in Sumatra and even in established wildlife reserves, poaching and the use of poison increased, stimulated by powerful commercial interests.

Destruction of the tiger's habitat

Meanwhile a much more important factor, which had been evident for some years, suddenly began to assume the proportions of a catastrophe. Throughout the tropical and subtropical regions of Asia the exploitation of hardwood forests was accelerating. The world demand for timber was sending prices through the roof. Not only in Asia, but in central Africa, Australasia and Central and South America, giant bulldozers and chain-saws were at work on a scale never seen before. By 1979 it was calculated that tropical forests were falling at a world-wide rate of fifty acres per *minute* and that by the year 2010 all the rain-forests of the world would be destroyed. In the mad scramble to benefit from the high prices, some contractors who had bought timber concessions were extracting only the eight largest trees per acre. All the rest were ruthlessly burnt in order to clear the ground. In the holocaust of fire which followed, every kind of wildlife perished if it could not flee. Among those which fled in Asia was the tiger, but it became increasingly difficult for it to find sanctuary.

The governments involved in this growing ecological catastrophe were at first able to condone it in the belief that the sooner the forests were cleared the sooner would new agricultural land become available. Unfortunately, as ecologists forecast, this was not so. Tropical rain forests, although constantly evolving, have maintained an almost continuously closed leaf

92 and 93. Millions of hungry cattle help to destroy Asia's forests by preventing the natural regeneration of trees. Goats are even more voracious and are the scourge of conservation.

canopy for anything up to sixty million years. Through this canopy very little, if any, sunlight ever penetrates to the gloom of the forest floor. The soil beneath is notoriously shallow and fragile, most of the nutrients being either very near the surface or stored in the vegetation. When such a forest is clear-felled and burnt, it is possible to grow crops for the first year or two in the soil which has been temporarily enriched by the wood-ash. But once exposed to the sun, the soil nutrients are oxidized and the heavy tropical rain washes the soil down into the valleys, where it can cause serious flooding by blocking water-courses. What remains is often little more than bare laterite, which will support no crop. Thus a once extremely vigorous and varied forest is converted into potential desert.

Tropical rain-forests are acknowledged to represent the richest genetic resource on earth. As such they are of incalculable value, not only to science, but to agriculture, arboriculture, medicine and animal husbandry. Although only a small part of these rich resources has yet been scientifically studied, they are being destroyed in one of the greatest ecological disasters ever perpetrated by man on his environment. Fortunately, in many parts of the world, scientists are now working closely with governments concerned, to improve the techniques of deforestation, so that the land can be converted to useful grazing or crop-growing. Moreover, the I.U.C.N. and the World Wildlife Fund are convincing more and more governments to preserve substantial parts of the various types of rain-forest as protected wildlife reserves.

Nonetheless, the fact remains that at the time this book went to press south-east Asia, the home of the tiger, had already lost more than half its tropical forests and that, according to the Food and Agriculture Organization, only 14 per cent of India's forests remain, 24 per cent of Thailand's and a mere 9.3 per cent of Bangladesh's. Malaysia lost 41.5 per cent in only ten years.

A second not inconsiderable factor leading to the destruction of the tiger's habitat in Asia was the devastation of forests during the wars in Korea and Vietnam. The United States Air Force dropped millions of dollars' worth of napalm and arsenical defoliants and huge quantities of bombs and shells on several thousand square miles of forest; and since the American withdrawal artillery and mortar shells have continued to fall on the forests of Laos, Cambodia and Thailand.

Thus, as a factor in the tiger's fight for survival, hunting has been far outstripped by the widespread destruction of habitat. Many tigers seeking cover or their own kind were shot in the open. Deprived of shelter and food, they retreated into smaller and smaller groups which, in Burma and in some parts of India for instance, are now so isolated that they can no longer be regarded as genetically viable breeding populations. Even though they are now protected, they will eventually degenerate and die out unless they can be moved to join other, larger groups, where they can re-establish an adequate gene-flow. This may perhaps be possible in India, but it is impossible with the very small Javan group as no others of this race exist in the wild and there is only one in captivity. Had it not been for 'Operation Tiger', which is described in the next chapter, it was clear by 1969 that the tiger species of all races was heading for extinction.

In 1930 it was believed that there were still at least 100,000 tigers of the eight races in various parts of Asia. At that time, although concern was being expressed about the decline in numbers of the Indian race, the others were thought to be secure, even though no reliable information was available concerning several of them. Nobody could foresee the future of the Asian forests. By 1940 the disappearance of the tiger from many of its old haunts in India had become so obvious that a rather ineffectual attempt was made to assess the size of the population. It is no longer clear how this was done, but a figure of 40,000 eventually emerged for the Indian race. Such a figure did not sound too bad and as India was by then actively embroiled in World War II the matter was dropped.

The long turmoil of Partition followed the war and although Indian tiger experts such as Kailash Sankhala, Billy Arjan Singh and B. Seshadri were well aware that the population decline was not only continuing but accelerating, their calls for effective action went unheeded.

As a result of wildlife expeditions which I led in 1966 and 1967 in Pakistan and in East Pakistan (later Bangladesh), I learned more about the plight of the tiger, in which I took an increasing interest. In 1968 I contacted all the tiger specialists I could locate in Europe and Asia (including the USSR) and began to piece together all the information available about the status of the various races. In this I received much valuable help from experts at the International Union for Conservation of Nature in Switzerland and particularly from Professor Paul Leyhausen, the chairman of the group of specialists in the world's cats.

Could the tiger be saved?

In 1969 the I.U.C.N. held its international congress in New Delhi. Along with Sankhala, Seshadri, Futehally and several others, I lobbied as many delegates as possible, to impress on them the need for action to be taken to save the Indian tiger, which at that time was not even listed as an endangered species in the famous I.U.C.N. Red Books, the definitive 'bibles' on which all nations now base their conservation programmes in relation to species of endangered fauna and flora. Until a species appears in the first category of a Red Book it is not officially regarded as in danger of becoming extinct.

As Sankhala, who was at that time Director of the Delhi Zoological Park, had succeeded in getting the tiger on the agenda, he was the obvious choice as our spokesman, a role he played with passionate conviction. He declared that the population of tigers in India had crashed to the appallingly low level of not more than two or three thousand and called on Mrs Gandhi's government to take immediate action to give them effective protection. I followed him and urged that the least the congress could do would be to vote that the Indian race of the tiger should be included in the appropriate Red

94. A tiger cub resting.

Book, as it was now quite obviously endangered. The motion was carried.

The Indian government responded, first by instructing all the State governments to make local provision for protecting tigers and later by passing legislation banning all tiger-hunting. Stimulated by this example and by recommendations made by the I.U.C.N. and World Wildlife Fund, other national governments gradually followed suit.

It is, however, one thing to pass laws and quite another to enforce them in countries where the law is held in little respect and which are subject to frequent changes of government. Nevertheless, within five years the tiger was given legal protection in every country where it occurred except China, Burma and the nations still at war. This was the essential first step in the coming battle to save the tiger.

At the New Delhi congress it was evident that a widespread lack of accurate information was the chief stumbling-block in obtaining action. Delegates from some countries still believed that tigers were plentiful and that protecting them would arouse social problems, particularly in regions where bounties were still being paid, not only for tigers shot, but also as compensation for cattle they had killed.

On returning to Europe I urged the I.U.C.N. and the World Wildlife Fund to mount an international fund-raising and propaganda campaign to save the tiger. As I expected, the scientists were reluctant to take any action until the true status of the various races could be ascertained. Some were still listed in I.U.C.N. records as 'population size and geographical distribution unknown'. The world-wide demands for help from both organizations were so great that they very properly insisted on giving priority to projects which were adequately documented, which mine was not. My proposal was turned down, partly for this reason and partly because I could give no assurance that the governments concerned would co-operate.

Further delay, I felt, might be fatal. Determined to persist, I wrote again to all my contacts in Asia, asking for the latest estimates of the status of the various tiger races. This produced only a small improvement to the statistical background material.

Shortly afterwards I heard from Zafar Futehally, the Indian representative of the I.U.C.N. and secretary of the Indian branch of the W.W.F., that a census of tigers was to be carried out for the Indian Board for Wildlife by the Department of Forests, under the direction of a skilled research officer, Dr S. R. Choudhury. Regular transects through all forests containing tigers were to be made, and all sightings, kills, vocalizations, tracks and defecations were to be recorded. In order to reduce duplication, the left hind pug-mark of each track was to be traced on a piece of framed ground-glass for comparison later. Male and female tigers have distinctly different pug-marks and there is a variation visible to a skilled tracker between the imprint of each tiger.

This was great news and I knew that at last accurate information about tigers in India would become available. When it did so, it astounded everyone. It revealed that only 1,827 tigers, plus or minus 10 per cent, now remained in the whole of India. If proof were needed that the tiger was

95–97. Skilled trackers can recognize individual tigers by their pug marks. The left-hand rear footprints are traced for comparison with existing records. Those of the front feet tend to be slightly distorted by their forward thrust.

98. *A tiger sleeping, in spite of the flies on its face.*

approaching extinction, there it was. Recognizing the difficulty of obtaining similarly accurate figures for the other races, I decided to concentrate first on saving the Indian tiger, in the hope that the others might be tackled later.

The distribution of the Indian race spread over India and Bangladesh to the three small kingdoms of Nepal, Sikkim and Bhutan and to western Burma as far as the Irrawaddy River. I already had approximate estimates for all but Burma and Sikkim (which is a tiny country) and could therefore now make a reasonable guess at the probable total size of the population of the Indian race, as follows:

India		1,827
Bangladesh	about	100
Nepal	about	150
Sikkim	a few	—
Bhutan	perhaps	200
West Burma	a few	—
TOTAL, say		2,400

A few years later it was discovered that the estimates for Nepal and Bangladesh were too low, but at the time they were accepted and served their purpose.

Our knowledge concerning the other races remained extremely vague.

99. A Siberian tiger in threatening posture in the Peking Zoo.

100. An aggressive Siberian tiger peering through the undergrowth. It takes large prey such as moose or the Manchurian wapiti.

The Russians said that about 130 Siberian tigers survived in the Sikhote Aline reserves in Manchuria, but we did not know whether there were others elsewhere in the Soviet Far East, or perhaps over the frontier in northern China. No information whatever was obtainable in those days about the Chinese race, although it was suspected that a few might still exist in northern Szechwan or the remoter parts of the Yangtse valley. The Indo-Chinese tiger had an enormous range; we knew that a few hundred existed in Thailand and peninsular Malaya, but could only guess at the number in eastern Burma and other countries in south-east Asia.

Strenuous efforts had been made to learn about the Caspian race, but none could be found in southern Russia, the Elburz mountains in Iran, nor in eastern Turkey. Pug-marks of a possible Caspian tiger were reported on the banks of the Oxus in Afghanistan, but neither there nor in its old haunts in the northern tugai forests of the upper Amu Dar'ya and Pyandzh basin were any found. This race seemed to be extinct.

The Sumatran tiger was known to be fairly numerous in the dense western and southern forests of the island, but these forests were disappearing and the large numbers of tiger-skins being shipped to Singapore and Hong Kong suggested that they would not last long. The population was thought to be 'about 400'. Finally there were the two other island races—the Javan and the Balinese. The former survived only in the Meru Betiri forest at the eastern end of this densely over-crowded island, where it was thought that its population had fallen from twenty-five in 1955 to between five and ten animals. It is strange that although Javan natives firmly believe tigers to be reincarnations of their own dead relatives, they have hunted them to the verge of extinction. On Bali, a much smaller and intensively cultivated island, nobody could say for certain whether any Balinese tigers survived. A few years later I visited Bali and satisfied myself that this race is now extinct. There is simply no forest left large enough to provide a tiger with food or shelter.

By 1970 therefore, the status of the eight races appeared to be as follows:

Siberian Tiger *P.t. altaica*	Perhaps 130
Chinese Tiger *P.t. amoyensis*	Perhaps a few
Indo-Chinese Tiger *P.t. corbetti*	Perhaps 2,000
Indian Tiger *P.t. tigris*	About 2,400
Caspian Tiger *P.t. virgata*	Probably extinct
Sumatran Tiger *P.t. sumatrae*	Perhaps 400–500
Javan Tiger *P.t. sondaica*	Between 5 and 10
Balinese Tiger *P.t. balica*	Extinct

So a species that had once dominated Asia, and of which probably 100,000 still remained in 1930, had in forty years been reduced by man to about 5,000 individuals scattered in small groups over an area larger than the whole of Europe. The Balinese and the Caspian races had been exterminated completely during this period, and the Javan and perhaps the Chinese races had also been driven to the brink of extinction.

In a way, this tragedy was more remarkable, although no less reprehensible, than the near extermination of the American buffalo. Although infinitely more numerous than the tiger, the buffalo (more correctly bison) was gregarious, moving in vast herds across the prairie in daylight. It could be slaughtered without difficulty by hunters on foot, on horseback, or, as happened later, from the comfort of a prairie train. The tiger was solitary, largely nocturnal and difficult to kill in the jungle. Only the deliberate destruction of its habitat could finally bring about its downfall. There were excuses, which were acceptable at the time, for the slaughter of a million buffaloes – to deprive the American Indians of their meat and hides. What excuses could we now make for so nearly depriving the world of its most beautiful tropical animal? Or could we, at the last minute, still save it?

Back from the Brink

I was convinced that there was still a fair chance of saving at least the Indian race, which the world knew best as the 'Royal Bengal Tiger', providing that three conditions were fulfilled. First, the scientific resources of the I.U.C.N. would have to be brought to bear on the techniques involved in such a difficult operation. Second, the willing co-operation of the governments concerned would have to be obtained. Third, the considerable cost of such a multi-national effort would have to be underwritten by the World Wildlife Fund.

I had taken negotiations concerning the first and third conditions as far as I could. The task now centred on the second and I therefore set out to see whether I could interest the heads of state in my proposals. I knew from previous negotiations that I had undertaken on behalf of the World Wildlife Fund, that if I could obtain the backing of the head of state, all doors would be open to me when it came to working out the details with government departments; whereas if I opened negotiations at lower levels I was often frustrated by bureaucracy.

My first visit was to Mrs Indira Gandhi, the Indian Prime Minister. With me were Charles de Haes, now Director General of the W.W.F., and Zafar Futehally, now Vice-President of W.W.F. India. I knew that Mrs Gandhi had inherited a deep interest in wildlife from her father Pandit Jawaharlal Nehru. She said she had seen me on television the previous night and was therefore aware of my interest in the tiger, which she regarded as a national symbol of India.

Seizing this opening, I outlined my proposals. If the Indian government were to support us and would also create a number of special reserves in areas where tigers were still relatively numerous, the I.U.C.N. would help in drafting plans for their scientific management and the necessary research. Also the W.W.F. would raise the equivalent of a million dollars (£400,000 at

101. A tigress and nearly full-grown cub on a tree trunk. It is not unusual to see a tigress with only one cub, the rest of the litter having been lost. Cubs do not leave their mother until they have two years' tuition in hunting.

102. Sultan Tipu of Mysore, defeated by the British in 1799, hated all Europeans. His favourite mechanical toy showed a tiger eating one. Simulated screams are produced by turning the handle.

that time) so that the reserves could be equipped to the highest standards. Although it was impossible to save all the tigers elsewhere in India, if these reserves were established and effective legislation against poaching and the black-market export of skins were enforced, the tiger could still be saved from extinction. De Haes, with his wisdom in negotiations of this kind, was quick to remark that such a programme could only succeed if directed and co-ordinated by the highest authority.

To my delight, the Prime Minister agreed without hesitation. 'I shall form a special committee – a Tiger Task Force,' she said, 'and it will report to me personally.'

A little stunned by the speed of her decision, I asked tentatively if I might repeat this at my press conference that evening. 'Certainly,' she replied.

India takes the initiative

The Tiger Task Force was appointed the next day. The chairman was Dr Karan Singh, one of India's most dynamic politicians and at that time Minister of Tourism and Civil Aviation. My old friend Kailash Sankhala was put in charge of implementing the programme, which later came to be called 'Project Tiger'. Zafar Futehally served as the link with the I.U.C.N. and W.W.F. Field surveys were made and a list of reserves proposed. A six-year plan, involving the expenditure of no less than £2,300,000 ($5,900,000) was approved by the government. A further budget that extended the programme until 1984 was approved later, nearly doubling the original figure. Bearing in mind India's tremendous economic and social problems, this set a magnificent example to the rest of Asia.

Before moving on to Bangladesh I attended a big press conference convened by Dr Karan Singh. In the course of a splendid speech, he said, 'During the hundred years of the British Raj, Englishmen slaughtered our tigers. Now an Englishman is leading a crusade to save them.' I thought this rather a wry comment even though justified by history. However, it was said with a smile.

In Dacca, capital of the new state of Bangladesh (formerly East Pakistan), I quickly obtained a meeting first with the new President, Justice Abu Syed Choudhury, and then with Prime Minister Sheikh Mujibur Rahman, the leader of the revolution which had succeeded, with India's aid, in gaining independence from Pakistan. Everyone was still in a state of euphoria over the victory, as well as being shocked at the devastation that it had brought. I feared that I could expect little interest in the tiger.

Nevertheless, the President welcomed my plans, saying that Bangladesh must take every opportunity to gain any international assistance which could restore the country to a normal condition. Moreover, the creation of wildlife reserves would help to attract tourism and foreign currency. He promised his support, adding rather sadly that the country's natural beauty was one of its few assets to have survived the war. This was a promising beginning, but I knew that real power lay with Mujibur Rahman and that without his backing I might still fail.

I met him that evening, having pushed my way through a milling throng of officials, journalists and petitioners to the ministerial offices. Press photographers were playing with a young leopard which someone had presented to the Prime Minister. The atmosphere was chaotic and very different from Mrs Gandhi's quietly efficient surroundings.

We were being served the inevitable tea when the Prime Minister burst in, greeting us with complete informality. His secretary had warned us that he was always in a hurry. In fact, while we talked, he never stopped pacing up and down, radiating vitality and nervous energy.

I outlined my proposals again, this time against constant interruptions and questions. He obviously liked them. His face lit up and from then on he did most of the talking.

'Conservation is part of my plan,' he declared. 'The destruction of forests has been terrible! But do you know what I did? Two days after becoming Prime Minister I issued a decree forbidding the felling of any more trees and the killing of any more wild animals. The tiger? Why, it's now our national emblem and on our new bank notes! Of course we shall protect it. We shall have a great national park in the Sunderbans!'

His enthusiasm was wonderful. I began to understand how such a man could have broken through the apathy of the patient Bengali peasants and led them in a war to create a new nation. He also meant what he said. Within a few years we had not a national park, but three tiger reserves in the Bangladesh Sunderbans. Like India, Bangladesh also issued special postage stamps depicting the tiger. Poor Mujibur Rahman. Little could I know that he was soon to fall to a hail of assassin's bullets. A few years later, after I had been negotiating with President Daoud of Afghanistan on behalf of the World Wildlife Fund, he too was assassinated and I began to wonder if I carried around a jinx with me.

It was nine o'clock before we left Mujibur Rahman's office. Although I was exhausted after a week of constant meetings and press conferences in India, I now had to meet the Bangladeshi press to ensure that the campaign received good coverage. I then had to summarize the meeting for the local radio station, which I did against a background of shrill chatter and honking taxi horns which probably made it unintelligible.

Early next morning I was on my way to Nepal. As the snow-capped Himalayas appeared through the aircraft window, I felt again the familiar thrill which landing at Kathmandu always gives me. John Blower, the project manager of the local United Nations wildlife conservation programme and adviser to the Nepalese government, was there to meet me; so also was George Schaller, whom I had last seen at the other end of the Himalayas, when he was studying snow leopards in Chitral. We exchanged news as we sat over coffee in the sunshine.

The situation in Nepal had changed since my last visit. Previously I had been able to discuss conservation developments directly with HM King Mahendra. Now, alas, he had died. He had been succeeded by his son, HM King Birendra, whom I had not yet met.

103. A tiger walking through the grass in the early evening, prior to a night's hunting.

I dined that night with the British Ambassador, Sir Terence O'Brien, and Sir Edmund Hillary, who was just back from the Himalayas. Although the Ambassador tried to arrange an audience for me with the new king, none was forthcoming. The king was still in official mourning and very busy with Cabinet appointments, and could not see me for at least a week. By that time I had to be back in Switzerland to present my proposals for the tiger project at a joint meeting of the I.U.C.N. and W.W.F. I agreed to wait as long as possible, but meanwhile briefed John Blower, who would be involved in the implementation of the proposals if they were accepted. During the next few days I visited the Royal Chitwan National Park, to find out how its tigers were progressing, and discussed with John Blower the possibility of creating two new reserves at Sukla Phanta and Karnali, both of which I knew were excellent tiger areas. There was time also for John to take me in a light aircraft to examine the Mount Langtang area, which he wanted to turn into a national park because of its extraordinary beauty. We managed to land somewhat precariously in a stony valley at an altitude of 12,400 feet near some scampering yaks, just short of the Langtang glacier. I agreed enthusiastically with John's proposal, for the peaks and lakes in the surrounding area were truly superb.

Fortunately, it was not long before HRH Prince Bernhard, at that time President of the World Wildlife Fund, visited the new King of Nepal and succeeded in obtaining agreement to all our proposals. In addition the King's brother, HRH Prince Gyanendra, took charge of the whole conservation programme, which has made great progress ever since. Today Nepal has three splendid tiger reserves at Chitwan, Karnali and Sukla Phanta, and both Langtang and the Khumbu areas surrounding Mount Everest have become spectacular national parks.

104 and 105. (Below) *A young tiger enjoying the warmth of a convenient rock.* (Right) *A sudden noise arouses him.*

106. Tigers find the beautiful chital, or axis deer, an easy prey. The antlers of these deer are still covered in velvet.

I had previously visited the small Kingdom of Sikkim and satisfied myself that very few tigers were resident here. Bhutan certainly had tigers, particularly in the Manas forests, but was very difficult to enter, so I decided that both these countries would have to be tackled later. In any case, I now had to return to Switzerland for a joint meeting of I.U.C.N. and the W.W.F. At the meeting it was agreed that the tiger project should now be given top priority. The W.W.F. immediately organized a world-wide fund-raising campaign, to be called 'Operation Tiger', and to be carried out by all its national organizations. The I.U.C.N. meanwhile appointed some of its most highly qualified people to liaise with their Indian, Nepalese and Bangladesh counterparts in planning the creation and management of the tiger reserves. Some were to be entirely new; others already in existence were to be enlarged and improved.

The creation of an effective wildlife reserve is not simply a matter of erecting a fence around a protected area. The reserve has to be skilfully

107. A fire watchtower in the Kanha National Park.

planned and managed, and its wildlife constantly monitored. First the site has to be accurately surveyed to ascertain its geophysical features, vegetation and water resources. The populations of its major animal species have to be determined in order to calculate the biomass in relation to the available food sources and the maximum carrying capacity of the reserve. In the case of the tiger this means knowing the numbers and sex ratios of its prey species. If necessary the amount of land available for grazing and browsing may have to be increased if the tigers are to have sufficient food to prevent them from wandering outside the reserve. If the deer and pigs are too numerous they may have to be culled to prevent them from destroying their habitat.

Guards must be able to patrol the reserve effectively. This involves the construction of roads and guard huts. Watch towers and water for fire-fighting have to be available and wells may have to be dug. Guards have to be recruited, trained and properly equipped with uniforms, vehicles, firearms,

108. Young foresters in the Kanha National Park in India receiving instruction in anti-poaching techniques as part of the 'Operation Tiger' campaign.

binoculars and two-way radio sets for controlling poaching. The co-operation of the local police, forestry officials and neighbouring civic authorities has to be obtained. Sometimes, to satisfy local requirements, a properly controlled hunting area has to be established outside the reserve, where surplus game can be shot on a sustained yield basis. Finally a long-term management plan must be prepared to cover not only the reserve but the protective buffer zone around it. Here the willing co-operation of the villagers is essential.

New reserves can rarely be established without imposing some restrictions on local activity. When planning a reserve one has to give a high priority to problems involving human interests. In Malaysia and New Guinea, for example, it was found that small numbers of aboriginal people inhabited the rain forests where new wildlife reserves were to be created. As in neither country were they seriously depleting the wildlife, but were living in peaceable equilibrium with it, no attempt was made to remove them. These

109. A tiger, sedated for treatment, being carried into a Landrover.

reserves indeed now protect both the aborigines and wildlife as part of the same ecosystem.

But particularly in Asia, villages may have to be translocated, a matter which requires very careful handling if friction is to be avoided. Both India and Nepal have shown particular skill in this difficult task and by generous treatment have re-settled numerous villages in new sites. Arrangements have to be made to exclude domestic cattle, which occur in thousands in almost all new reserve sites. Those which enter after a reserve has been created are put in a pound and have to be reclaimed on payment of a nominal fine. In some reserves villagers are allowed entry for a few days each year to harvest essential fodder, firewood, thatching, fruit or wild honey, under a controlled programme. The annual burning of grass, which is usually a dangerously uncontrolled affair, has also to be strictly managed.

The creation of a wildlife reserve involves a considerable number of jobs for villagers in road-making, building, transporting, the hiring of elephants,

bullocks and boatmen and in miscellaneous labour. Moreover, unlike many enterprises run by remote city-dwellers or foreigners, the money earned continues to circulate locally, thus enriching the community.

After the reserve has started to operate, plans usually have to be made to cater for tourism. People cannot enjoy wildlife unless they can see it. But here again great care must be exercised. Uncontrolled tourism can destroy a reserve by sheer success and weight of numbers. In the United States, for example, only 350,000 people visited the already fully established national parks in 1916; by 1978 the number had risen to 45 million and restrictions had to be introduced to prevent serious disturbance and the destruction of vegetation by tourists. Tourism, however, generates local employment and is an important source of revenue that offsets the cost of managing and guarding a reserve.

When a new wildlife reserve is created full account must be taken of the social and economic needs of the human community if the reserve is to have an assured future. It must never be seen as detrimental to man. Conservation is invariably a compromise between the need to protect wildlife and the aspirations of the local human population. In Asia particularly, where the density of the population is so high and the economic problems so great, much skill and patience are needed in balancing these priorities.

'Operation Tiger' is launched

In September 1972 HRH Prince Bernhard launched Operation Tiger at an international press conference. The media gave us remarkably generous support. The tiger was a glamorous and news-worthy subject, and its plight aroused immediate popular interest. Prominent feature articles and pictures, television films and interviews rapidly multiplied.

Some remarkable efforts were made by our supporters to raise money. The most outstanding was the contribution of David Shepherd, the famous wildlife artist. He had already raised very large sums for the W.W.F. through the sale of his animal paintings and had recently presented a helicopter to President Kaunda of Zambia, for the control of elephant-poachers. He now painted a magnificent picture of a tiger, which he donated to the W.W.F. (see plate 111). His idea was that a limited edition of signed, full-size reproductions should be sold at £150 each for the benefit of the appeal. Despite the high price the demand for his work was so great that the entire edition of 850 copies was sold in six weeks. As some of them are now changing hands at three times this price they were obviously a good investment! After paying for the cost of reproduction, which was done at cost price by the generous printers, David handed over the proceeds, no less than £112,000, to the W.W.F. In recognition of his services to conservation, HRH Prince Bernhard later decorated him with his personal Order of the Golden Ark.

David Ogilvy, described as the world's leading advertising man and a member of the Executive Council of the W.W.F., put the full resources of his international company at our disposal and produced some compelling advertisements appealing for donations. These appeared in many countries,

110. A Siberian tiger walking down a slope.

111. David Shepherd painting 'Tiger Fire', prints of which raised £112,000 for 'Operation Tiger'.

112. A tiger guarding its prey. As in David Shepherd's painting of a snarling tiger, the ears are laid back and the nose wrinkled.

113. Advertisements such as this, paid for by benefactors, enabled the World Wildlife Fund to raise £800,000 for 'Operation Tiger', which saved the species from extinction.

the cost being borne either by the newspapers and magazines or by other donors.

Young people of many nations took an active interest in the campaign, buying 'Save the Tiger' T-shirts and collecting money. In Great Britain, Switzerland and the Netherlands the W.W.F. Youth Service raised the remarkable sum of £300,000. Some of the youngsters in the United States even took to hissing women who wore tiger-skin coats, so that very soon it became socially unacceptable to do so. In London a tiger-skin coat was burnt in public by one protest group. Several large multi-national companies which used the tiger as an advertising symbol made substantial donations to the fund and the officers and crew of H.M.S. *Tiger* also contributed. The Armed Services agreed to replace tiger-skin aprons worn by their ceremonial drummers with synthetic furs. The International Fur Trades Federation introduced a voluntary ban on the importation of tiger skins. Fashion houses

114. A tigress (centre) *with three nearly full-grown cubs. The third cub is just visible behind the one walking.*

co-operated by producing excellent imitations of many animal furs, which have since become very popular. Virtually every airline signed a W.W.F. agreement to stop advertising the hunting of tigers and other endangered species as a means of promoting air travel.

At about this time the I.U.C.N. achieved a major break-through for conservation. An international treaty it had prepared, the Convention on the International Trade in Endangered Species of Fauna and Flora, was adopted at a multi-national meeting convened by the United States Government. This made it illegal for any country to export or import, either alive or as skins, any animal species listed in the I.U.C.N. Red Books as endangered. The treaty has since been ratified by fifty-nine nations, including those where tigers occur.

115. A tiger lying well hidden in a shady spot after its meal.

As a result the once very large international trade in tiger skins has almost been wiped out.

In eighteen months the campaign raised nearly £800,000 ($1,700,000), the largest contributors being Switzerland, the United States, Great Britain and the Netherlands, in that order. Contributions had come from as far afield as South Africa and Australia and it was the most successful campaign yet organized by the W.W.F.

With this money the W.W.F. has already supplied about forty vehicles and two launches for the Sunderbans reserves, complete radio networks for all the reserves as well as tractors, fencing, camping and fire-fighting equipment, night viewing apparatus, telemetry and capture equipment,

116. A tiger drinking, keeping a watchful eye on the photographer.

117. A tiger with the carcass of a domestic buffalo.

elephants and camels, generators and water-pumps, projectors and laboratory equipment and uniforms, binoculars and arms for guards.

The money raised by 'Operation Tiger' has been well spent. In 1976 a mid-term appraisal of progress with the new reserves was carried out by Professor Paul Leyhausen and Dr Colin Holloway of the I.U.C.N. and Mr M.K. Ranjitsinh, the United Nations Environment Programme representative for Asia and the Far East. Their report stated that quite outstanding successes in furthering the tiger's chances of survival had already been achieved.

Only four years later, in 1980, there are reports that the numbers of tigers in all the established reserves have increased substantially. In one or two instances the population has even doubled, thanks to more successful breeding, the high standards of protection against poaching and, probably, to an influx of tigers from the unprotected regions outside the reserves. There has also been a remarkable increase in the populations of deer and

118. *A tiger has killed a small domestic calf which will be eaten in a single meal.*

119. *A tiger growling. Just out of sight is the carcass of its prey.*

120. (Left) *A tiger with a chital (axis deer).*

121. (Below) *A tigress carrying a hog deer which it has killed. In the pool, her nearly full-grown cub eagerly watches the arrival of the meal.*

antelope, as a result of the improved management of the grazing areas. Moreover, the reserves, which represent a total of many thousands of square miles of forest, are providing sanctuary for every kind of wildlife, from tigers and leopards and their prey species to wild elephants and rare birds, reptiles, butterflies and plants.

One important result of 'Operation Tiger' was that it quickly attracted the attention of other countries where tigers occur. Within a short time Malaysia, Thailand and Indonesia had expressed themselves willing to create new tiger reserves. Contact had also been established with HM King Jigme Singh-ye Wangchuh of Bhutan, who had created a big reserve in the Bhutan Manas forest adjoining the Indian Manas reserve. The two were put under joint management and now form one of the largest population centres for

122. Tiger cubs playing, an essential part of the learning process.

tigers. Fortunately sufficient funds were by then becoming available, although the extra demands on the tiger specialists at the I.U.C.N. became a problem.

In 1979 Sir Peter Scott, Chairman of the W.W.F., visited China, where he achieved another long awaited breakthrough for conservation. The Chinese government not only became members of the I.U.C.N., but also agreed to sign the Convention on the International Trade in Endangered Species. A wide-ranging programme of wildlife conservation was planned, including the creation of many new reserves. One surprise was to learn that about 150 tigers, reported to be of the Siberian race, existed in four reserves in the northern part of Heilungkiang Province. Since the Russians had recently announced that the number in their Sikhote Alin reserves had now risen to 150, this doubled the known population of the race. According to zoologists at the Academia Sinica in Peking, the Chinese tiger still existed in small numbers and is now protected. It is also believed locally that both the Indo-Chinese and Indian races of the tiger may still survive in the more remote western and southern parts of China. A very rewarding outcome of Sir Peter's visit was an invitation to send an expert from I.U.C.N. to make a two-year study of the now rare Chinese giant panda, of which perhaps only 400 exist in the wild. By a happy coincidence the panda is the symbol of the World Wildlife Fund.

The tiger is saved

Thanks partly to 'Operation Tiger', but chiefly to the wholehearted efforts of the various countries concerned, a large number of well-managed reserves are today providing the tiger with a real chance of survival. Their locations are as follows:

India

The Manas Reserve, in Assam.
The Palamau National Park, in Bihar.
The Simlipal Reserve, in Orissa.
The Corbett National Park, in Uttar Pradesh.
The Ranthambore Reserve, in Rajasthan.
The Sariska Reserve, in Rajasthan.
The Kanha National Park, in Madhya Pradesh.
The Melghat Reserve, in Maharashtra.
The Bandipur Reserve, in Karnataka.
The Sunderbans Reserve, in West Bengal.
The Jaldapara Reserve, in West Bengal.
The Periyar Reserve, in Kerala.

Bangladesh

Three reserves in the Sunderbans.

Nepal
The Royal Chitwan National Park.
The Royal Karnali Reserve.
The Royal Sukla Phanta Reserve.

Bhutan
The Bhutan Manas Reserve.

Malaya
The Tamang Neggara National Park.
The Krau Game Reserve, in Pahang.
A new reserve in Trengganu.

Thailand
The Khao Yai National Park.
The Khao Soi Daow Reserve.
The Huai Kha Khaeng Reserve.
The Tung Yai Reserve.
The Salak Pra Reserve.
The Phu Hkien Game Sanctuary.
The Phu Khiew Game Sanctuary.
Other reserves in formation.

Indonesia
The Meru Betiri Reserve, in Java.
The Gunung Leuser National Park, in Sumatra.
The Sumatera Selatan Reserve, in Sumatra.
Several new reserves in formation.

USSR
The Sikhote Alin Reserves, in Manchuria.
The Suputinsk Reserve, in Manchuria.
The Lazovsky Reserve, in Manchuria.

China
The Chang-bai Shan Reserve.
The Mengyan Reserve.
The Fangjinshan Reserve.
Other reserves in formation.

Korea
Several new reserves in formation.

The situation in Burma remains obscure, although it is known that both the Indian and Indo-Chinese races still survive there in spite of their lack of legal protection. Information is also still lacking from Vietnam, Cambodia and

Laos, in all of which some tigers probably still exist. News has, however, been recently received that at least 50 tigers of undetermined race (probably the Siberian) are now known to have survived in northern Korea.

In 1979 revised estimates of total populations of the eight races of the tiger (which should be compared with those of 1969, shown on page 87) were still partly guesswork, but were as follows:

Siberian Tiger *P.t. altaica*		350–400
Chinese Tiger *P.t. amoyensis*		small numbers?
Indo-Chinese Tiger *P.t. corbetti*		about 2,000
Indian Tiger *P.t. tigris*		about 3,300
Caspian Tiger *P.t. virgata*		extinct?
Sumatran Tiger *P.t. sumatrae*		600–800
Javan Tiger *P.t. sondaica*		1–2
Balinese Tiger *P.t. balica*		extinct
	Total	about 6,400

The numbers of the doomed Javan race have continued to fall. A survey made in 1979 could find no proof that the survivors were still breeding. Moreover, it seems that the small food sources available in the Meru Betiri reserve were subject to increasing competition from leopards and wild dogs.

Ten years previously there seemed little hope of saving the tiger species from total extinction. Today it can be said that the Indian, Indo-Chinese, Siberian and Sumatran races now have an excellent chance of long-term survival if the present measures for their protection are maintained. There is every hope that they will be, although poaching in Sumatra is not yet fully controlled.

Nevertheless, it would be unrealistic to deny that new problems are looming ahead. Many of the tiger reserves, particularly those in India, are only 200 to 400 square miles large and are therefore too small to sustain increasing populations for long. While some of them may successfully be enlarged, it will not be possible to extend the boundaries of others in more highly developed and crowded areas; perhaps their tiger population will be stabilized by natural means, but overcrowding brings heavy penalties. If this arises, tigers will have to be translocated, either to new reserves created in suitable areas of low human population density, or perhaps to the very few reserves large enough to accommodate additional numbers. Another obvious problem is to maintain an adequate gene-flow in small reserves. The I.U.C.N. scientists have already calculated that in order to maintain a viable breeding stock for an indefinite period, a minimum contiguous population of 300 tigers is required. Others believe that 200 would be sufficient. In the Indian subcontinent only the Sunderbans reserves in India and Bangladesh, the joint reserves in the Bhutan and Assam Manas forests and the joint Tung Yai and Huai Khaeng reserves have this capability. It may therefore become necessary to exchange a certain number of surplus tigresses between small reserves. Obviously tigers of the surviving races must not be intermixed.

Yet another problem is the over-spill of tigers from over-crowded reserves into the surrounding country. When this happens, domestic cattle are liable to be taken in the unprotected buffer-zone around reserves and people may be attacked. To calm the fears of villagers near tiger reserves, it has already been necessary to make arrangements for compensation to be paid quickly if any cattle are taken. Problems such as these rarely arise in countries where wildlife reserves are measured in thousands of square miles, but in densely populated Asia they are vitally important and will have to be watched very carefully by the reserve managers.

The question will probably be asked, 'Was it worthwhile and necessary to spend so much effort and money on preventing the extinction of the tiger, when so many other problems are facing humanity?' It is the kind of question which faces all conservationists.

The answer must be 'Yes'. If no effort were made to protect the natural world, humanity would be suffering far more than it does at present. Already, to our loss, we have caused the extinction of countless animals and plants. More than one thousand animal species of various kinds and twenty-five thousand species of plants are now listed as endangered. Each loss impoverishes our environment and weakens man's prospect of long-term survival by further unbalancing the ecosystem. We dominate this planet by our skill and technology, but still cannot escape the fact that all life is interdependent. The tiger has been referred to by an eminent scientist as a 'most sensitive indicator of the health of the natural area and the country at large'. This may perhaps sound far-fetched, but it is not. Like all other animals, the tiger has a part to play in its natural community. Remove it and the community is at once unbalanced – deer and pigs, for example, can multiply to excessive numbers, which in turn are able to increase their damage to man's crops. Saving the tiger and its forest habitat was not, however, merely a matter of preventing extra damage to crops in Asia. It was a remarkable demonstration, by a large number of relatively poor Third World countries, of their awareness of the importance of protecting their natural heritage. Can we in the affluent West question their decision to spend money and effort on such a cause? Was it wrong to hasten to help them achieve such a goal? I think we had a duty to do so, because, as the Prime Minister of India said at the 1979 Symposium, the tiger campaign 'was not just for the survival of our heritage of wildlife, but also for the survival of man'. And this, I believe, is the real answer to the question.

As for the cost involved, one has only to compare it with what the nations of the world are willingly spending on new weapons of destruction. In 1978 military expenditure amounted to £212,000 million ($530,000 million). Saving the tiger and its habitat will have cost, taking everything into account, less than the price of a single short-lived modern bomber aircraft. Or to put it another way, the equivalent of about the cost of seven miles of a six-lane highway. One may ask which of these represents the best long-term investment for humanity. The tiger is part of everyone's heritage and I, for one, am proud to have played a part in the crusade to save it.

123. Pugmarks in the sand at Sunderbans.

Selected Bibliography

Allen, H.: *The Lonely Tiger* (1960)
Ali, S.: *The Moghul Emperors of India as Naturalists and Sportsmen.* J. Bombay Nat. Hist. Soc., 31(4): 833–61 (1927)
Anon.: *Poison for Indian Tigers and Leopards,* Oryx 8(2) 1965
Baikov, N.: *The Manchurian Tiger* (1925)
Baker, S.: *Wild Beasts and their Ways* (1890)
Baze, W.: *Tiger! Tiger!* (1957)
Bolton, M.: *Royal Chitawan National Park Management Plan 1975–79* (1975)
Boswell, K.: *'Scent trails' and 'pooking' in tiger,* J. Bombay Nat. Hist. Soc., 54(2): 452–54 (1957)
Brahmachary, R. L. and Dutta, J.: *Phenylethylamine as a Biochemical Marker of Tiger.* Zeitschrift für Naturforschung: 632–3 (1979)
—— *On the Pheromones of Tigers.* American Naturalist – in press (1980)
Brander, A.: *Wild Animals of Central India* (1923)
Burton, R. G.: *The Book of the Tiger* (1933)
—— *The Tiger Hunters* (1936)
Champion, F.: *With a Camera in Tiger-land* (1927)
Cooch Behar, Maharajah of: *Thirty-seven Years of Big Game Shooting* (1908)
Corbett, J.: *Man-eaters of Kumaon* (1944)
—— *Man-eaters of India* (1957)
Crandall, L.: *The Management of Wild Animals in Captivity* (1964)
Dang, H.: *The Future of the Tiger.* The Chital 5(1): 46–47 (1962)
Denis, A.: *Cats of the World* (1964)
Dollman, G. and Burlace, J.: *Rowland Ward's Records of Big Game* (1935)
Ewer, R. F.: *The Carnivores* (1973)
Fisher, J., Simon, N. and Vincent, J.: *The Red Book – Wildlife in Danger* (1969)
Fitter, R. and Leigh-Pemberton, J.: *Vanishing Wild Animals of the World* (1968)
Gee, E. P.: *Albinism and partial Albinism in Tigers.* J. Bombay Nat. Hist. Soc., 56(3): 581–587 (1959)
—— *The Wildlife of India* (1964)
Gilbert, R.: *Notes on man-eating Tigers.* J. Bombay Nat. Hist. Soc., 4(3): 195–206 (1899)
Gupta, A.: *Tigers at high altitudes.* J. Bengal Nat. Hist. Soc., 29(1): 55–56 (1959)
Hicks, F. C.: *Forty Years among the Wild Animals of India* (1910)
Holloway, C. W., Leyhausen, P. and Ranjitsinh, M. K.: *Conservation of the Tiger in India.* I.U.C.N. (1976)
Indian Board for Wildlife (Government of India): *Project Tiger* (1972)
Jackson, P. F. R.: *Bali Tiger Extinct?* Defenders of Wildlife 50 (1): 34. (1975)
—— *Scientists hunt the Bengal Tiger.* Smithsonian Mag. (1978)
—— *Tiger Men report to World Meeting.* Wildlife News 3 (1979)
Jerdon, T.: *The Mammals of India* (1874)
Kleiman, D. G.: *The Estrous Cycle of the Tiger.* In 'The World's Cats' 2: 60–75 (1974)
Lekagul, B. and McNeely, J. A.: *The Mammals of Thailand* (1977)
Leyhausen, P.: *Verhaltensstudien an Katzen* (1960)
—— *The Communal Organization of Solitary Mammals* (1965)
Locke, A.: *The Tigers of Trengganu* (1954)
Lydekker, R.: *The Game Animals of India, Burma, Malaya and Tibet* (1924)
Matjushkin, E. N., Zhivotchenko, V. I. and Smirnov, E. N.: *The Tiger in the U.S.S.R.* I.U.C.N. (1977)
McDougal, C.: *The Face of the Tiger* (1977)
McDougal, C. and Seidensticker, J.: *The Tigers of Mohan Khola* (1976)
Medway, Lord: *The Wild Mammals of Malaya* (1969)
Mishra, H. R.: *Annual Report (1978–9) The Nepal Tiger Ecology Project* (MSS.)
Morris, D.: *The Mammals* (1965)
Mountfort, G.: *The Vanishing Jungle* (1969)
—— *The Bengal Tiger enters the Red Book.* Animals 13(3): 110–112 (1970)
—— *Tigers* (1973)
—— *International Efforts to save the Tiger.* Biol. Cons. 6: 48–52 (1974)
—— *Back from the Brink.* (1978)
Novikov, G.: *Carnivorous Mammals of the Fauna of the U.S.S.R.* (1962)
O'Brien, E.: *Where man-eating Tigers occur.* J. Bombay Nat. Hist. Soc., 45(1): 231–2 (1944)
Perry, R.: *The World of the Tiger* (1964)
Pocock, R.: *The Fauna of British India: Mammals* (1939)
Powell, A.: *The Call of the Tiger* (1957)
Prater, S.: *The Book of Indian Animals* (1948)
Qianzhu, X. and Jing, Z.: *The Tiger and its Conservation in China.* Report to Int. Tiger Symposium (1979)
Rice, W.: *Tiger-shooting in India* (1857)
Sankhala, K.: *Breeding Behaviour of the Tiger in Rajasthan.* Int. Zoo Yearbook 7: 133–147 (1967)
—— *The Vanishing Indian Tiger.* I.U.C.N. Tech. Report 18(2): 34–45 (1970)
—— *Tiger.* World Wildlife Fund (1974)
—— *Tigerland* (1975)
Schaller, G.: *My Year with the Tigers.* Life 58(25): 60–66 (1965)
—— *The Deer and the Tiger.* (1967)
Seidensticker, J.: *On the Ecological Separation between Tigers and Leopards* (1976)
Seshadri, B.: *The Twilight of India's Wildlife* (1969)
—— *New Hope for the Tiger.* Country Life 154: 1714–16 (1973)
Simon, N. et al.: *Red Data Book (1) Mammalia.* I.U.C.N. (1966)
Simon, N. and Geroudet, P.: *Last Survivors* (1970)
Singh, A.: *Status and Social Behaviour of the North Indian Tiger.* In 'The World's Cats' (1): 176–188 (1973)
—— *Tiger Haven* (1975)
Singh, K.: *The Tiger of Rajasthan* (1959)
Smith, J. L. D.: *Smithsonian Tiger Ecology Project Report No. 13* (1978)
Smith, J. L. D. and Tamang, K. M.: *Smithsonian Tiger Ecology Project Report No. 2* (1977)
Sunquist, M. E.: *The Movements and Activities of Tigers in Royal Chitawan National Park, Nepal.* Ph.D. Thesis (1979)
Sunquist, M. E., Tamang, K. M. and Troth, R. G.: *Smithsonian Tiger Ecology Project Report No. 11* (1976)
Somerville, A.: *The Home of the Man-eater* (1933)
Sterndale, R.: *Natural History of Indian Mammals* (1884)
Stacey, P.: *The Future of the Tiger.* Chital 3(2): 29–32 (1961)
Talbot, L.: *A look at threatened species.* Fauna Pres. Soc. (1960)
Tamang, K. M.: *Population Characteristics of the Tiger and its Prey.* (1979)
Waller, R.: *Last chance for the Tiger?* Animals 13(16): 748–51 (1971)

Scientific names of the species

Bear, Himalayan Black *Selanarctos thibetanus*
Bear, Sloth *Melurus ursinus*
Bison, American *Bison bison*
Blackbuck *Antilope cervicapra*
Buffalo, Water *Bubalus bubalis*
Cat, Desert *Felis libyca*
Cat, Jungle *Felis chaus*
Chevrotain (Mouse Deer) *Tragulus javanicus*
Crocodile, Marsh *Crocodilus palustris*
Deer, Barasingha *Cervus duvauceli*
Deer, Barking *Muntiacus muntjak*
Deer, Chital *Axis axis*
Deer, Hog *Hyelaphus porcinus*
Deer, Musk *Moschus moschiferus*
Deer, Roe *Capriolus capriolus*
Deer, Sambur *Cervus unicolor*
Deer, Sika *Cervus nippon*
Dhole (Wild Dog) *Cuon alpinus*
Elephant, Indian *Elaphus maximus*
Gaur *Bos gaurus*
Gorilla, Mountain *Gorilla gorilla*
Hyena, Striped *Hyaena hyaena*
Jackal, Asiatic *Canis aureus*
Leopard, *Panthera pardus*
Leopard, Clouded *Neofelis nebulosa*
Leopard, Snow *Panthera uncia*
Lion, African *Panthera leo*
Lynx *Felis lynx*
Moose *Alces alces*
Panda, Giant *Ailuropoda melanoleuca*
Peafowl *Parvo cristatus*
Pig, Wild *Sus scrofa*
Porcupine, Indian Crested *Hystrix indica*
Python, Rock *Python molurus*
Rhinoceros, Indian *Rhinoceros unicornis*
Tiger, Balinese *Panthera tigris balica*
Tiger, Caspian *Panthera tigris virgata*
Tiger, Chinese *Panthera tigris amoyensis*
Tiger, India *Panthera tigris tigris*
Tiger, Indo-Chinese *Panthera tigris corbetti*
Tiger, Javan *Panthera tigris sondaica*
Tiger, Sabre-toothed *Smilodon*
Tiger, Siberian *Panthera tigris altaica*
Tiger, Sumatran *Panthera tigris sumatrae*
Vulture *Gyps sp.*
Wapiti, Manchurian *Cervus elaphus xanthopygus*
Yak *Bos grunniens*

Acknowledgements

The author and John Calmann & Cooper Ltd. would like to thank the following photographers who provided the photographs for this book:
Ardea: Charles McDougal 9, 34, 49, 77, 94, 98; Richard Waller 68; 109, 116
Tony Beamish: 89.
Bildagentur Adolf Schmidecker: 70, 101, 122.
British Museum (Department of Natural History): 5.
Bruce Coleman Inc.: George Schaller 72.
Bruce Coleman Ltd.: Dieter and Mary Plage 2, 118; Gordon Langsbury 58.
Sven Gahlin: 88.
John Hillelson Collection: W. W. Hooper 84, 85.
George Holton: 100.
Jacana: Collection Varin-Visage, 8.
Peter Jackson: 3, 6, 11–13, 15, 16, 24–29, 33, 36, 38–45, 48, 50, 51, 53, 55, 59, 61, 69, 71, 74, 75, 80, 91–93, 96, 97, 99, 107, 108, 110, 117, 123.
Keystone Press Agency: 62.
Mansell Collection: 87.
Hugh Maynard: 32.
Guy Mountfort: 18, 19, 47, 54, 95.
Charles McDougal: 31, 37.
Pictor International: frontispiece.
Photo Researchers Ltd.: K. S. Sankhala 10, 14, 35, 73, 79; Dhiraj Chawda 52; E. Ranumantha Rao 56.
Harry Teyn: 4, 57, 64, 67.
Valmik Thapar, Fateh Singh, Tejbir Singh: 17, 20–23, 30, 78, 82, 83, 103–106, 114, 115, 119, 120.
Victoria and Albert Museum: 86, 102.
World Wildlife Fund: John Blower 46, 76; Peter Jackson 60; M. Y. Ghorpdale 90, 111, 113, 121.
Zoological Society of Great Britain: Michael Lyster 65, 66; 63.

Index

Page numbers in *italic* refer to Captions

Academia Sinica 113
Afghanistan 15, 17, 86
Amu Dar'ya River 86
Aral Sea 15
Aspinall, John 48
Assam 115
Azerbaijan 15

Baker, Stuart 60
Bali 15, 87
Bangladesh 8, 12, 65, 67, 79, 80, 84, 91, 92, 113, 115
Bear, Himalayan black 37
  Sloth 37, 70
Bengal, Bay of 25, 65
Bergmann's Rule 15
Bernhard, H.R.H. Prince 94, 101
Bhopal, Maharajah of 74
Bhutan 15, 84, 96, 111, 114, 115
Birendra, H.M. King 93, 94
Bison, American 87
Blackbuck 25
Blower, John 92, 93, 94
Bose Research Institute 46
Brahmachary, Dr R. L. 46
Brahmaputra River 65
Buffalo, domestic 10, *26*, *27*, *31*, 32, 57, 58, 70, *108*
Burma 13, 81, 84, 86, 114

Cambodia 75, 79, 114
Caspian Sea 15, 76
Cat, desert 48
  jungle 48
Cattle, domestic 28, *30*, 78, 99, *109*, 116
Ceylon 15
China 13, 76, 81, 86, 113, 114
Chitral 92
Chittagong Hill Tracts 37
Chitwan National Park 12, *36*, 38, 44, 60, 93, 94, 114
Choudhury, Chief Justice Abu Syed 91
Choudhury, Dr S. L. 62, 82
Churia Hills 45
Convention on the International Trade in Endangered Species 104, 113
Corbett, Jim 75
Corbett National Park 75, 113
Crocodile, marsh 37
Curzon, Lord *74*

Dacca 91
Daoud, President 92
Deer, barasingha 27, *28*, 67
  barking 25
  chevrotain 25
  chital *24*, 28, 40, 45, 67, *96*, *111*
  hog 25, *111*
  musk 44
  roe 44
  sambur *24*, 27, 32, 40
  sika 44
Delhi, New 80, 82; Zoological Park 80
Dhole (wild dog) *37*, 52, 115
Durian 25
Dutta, Dr J. 46

Elburz Mountains 86
Elephant, Indian 10, 25, 37, 40, 111
Everest, Mount 94
Food and Agriculture Organization (F.A.O.) 7, 79
Forests, destruction of 77–9, 86
Futehally, Zafar 9, 80, 82, 89, 91

Gandhi, Mrs Indira 80, 89, 91, 92, 116
Ganges River, Plain 38, 65
Gaur 25, *31*, 32, 37
George V, H.M. King 70
Gland 67
Gloger's Rule 15
Goats *35*, *78*
Govindgarh 22
Great Britain 103, 105
Gyanendra, H.R.H. Prince 94

Haes, Charles de 89, 91
Harappa Civilization 68
Hendricks, Dr Herbert 67
Hillary, Sir Edmund 93
Himalayas 15, 16, 17, 38, 92, 93
H.M.S. *Tiger* 8, 103
Holloway, Dr Colin 108
Hong Kong 86
Hyderabad 70
Hyena, striped 52

Indian, government of 22, 80, 81, 89, 91
Indian Board for Wildlife 82
Indian Statistical Institute 46
Indian Tiger Project 62
Indo-China 13
Indonesia 111
Indus River 15, 68
International Fur Trades Federation 103
International Union for Conservation of Nature and Natural Resources (I.U.C.N.) 7, 67, 79, 80, 81, 82, 89, 91, 93, 96, 104, 108, 113, 115
Iran 15, 86
Irrawaddy River 84

Jackal 28, 52, 75
Jackson, Peter 9
Java 15, 79, 87

Kanha National Park 10, 12, *13*, 60, *97*, *98*, 113
Karnali Reserve 93, 94, 114
Kathmandu 92
Kaunda, President 101
Khulna 65
Khumbu 94
Korea 76, 114, 115
Korean War 62, 79

Langtang, Mount 94
Langur monkey *32*
Laos 79, 115
Leopard *35*, 37, 40, 52, 70, 111, 115
  clouded 13
  snow 92
Leyhausen, Prof. Paul 9, 80, 108
Lion, African 23, 48, 51, 52, 59
Lyns 48

Macaque monkey *32*
Madhya Pradesh 10
Mahendra, H.M. King 92
Malaysia (Malaya) 13, 25, 79, 86, 98, 111, 114
Manas Reserves 96, 111, 113–14, 115
Manchuria 44, 86, 114
Mandla 60
McDougal, Dr Charles 9, 12, 32, 38, 48, 50, 51, 53, *62*
Meru Betiri Reserve 86, 114, 115
Miquelle, Dale 38
Mishra, Himanta 38
Moghuls 68
Moose, Manchurian 44, *86*
Nehru, Pandit Jawaharlal 89
Nepal 8, 12, 15, *36*, *62*, 70, 84, 92, 94, 99, 114
Netherlands 103, 105
New Guinea 98
Nightingale, Col. 70
Nilgai *30*
Novikov, G. 44

O'Brien, Sir Terence 93
Ogilvy, David 101
Oxus River 86

Pakistan 15, 80, 91
Pamir Mountains 15
Panda, Giant 113
Peafowl 32
Pig, wild *24*, 37, 44, 57, 67, 116
Porcupine, Indian *25*, 37
Pyandzh Basin 86
Python 52

Rahman, Sheikh Mujibur 91, 92
Rai, Prem Badahur 44–5
Ranjitsinh, M. K. 108
Rapti river 38
Reserves, list of 113–14
Rewa, Maharajah of 22
Rhinoceros, Indian one-horned *25*, 37, 40
Rice, W. 70

Sankhala, Kailash 9, 12, 80, 91
Schaller, Dr George 9, 12, 32, 48, 51, 53, 56, 70, 92
Scott, Sir Peter 7, 113
Seidensticker, Dr John C. 38, *41*
Seshadri, B. 80
Shepherd, David 101, *102*
Sikhote Alin Reserves 86, 113, 114
Sikkim 84, 96
Singapore 86
Singh, Arjan 9, 80
Singh, Dr Karan 91
Siwalik Hills 75
Smith, Dr J. L. D. 9, 38
Smithsonian Institution 38
Sukla Phanta Reserve 93, 94, 114
Sumatra 15, 16, 75, 77, 114, 115
Sunderbans 12, 16, 62, 65, 67, 92, 105, 113, 115, 116
Sunquist, Dr Melvyn 38
Surguja, Maharajah of 70
Switzerland 67, 80, 93, 96, 103, 105

Taiwan 75
Tamang, Kirti Man 38
Telemetry, use of 38–41, *43*
Thailand 75, 79, 86, 111, 114
Tibet 15
Tiger, Balinese 13, 15, 86, 87, 115
  Caspian 13, 16, 76, 86, 87, 115
  Chinese 13, 15, 76, 86, 87, 113, 115
  Indian 13, 15, *17*, *53*, 84, 87, 89, 113, 114, 115
  Indo-Chinese 13, *46*, 87, 113, 114, 115
  Javan 13, 15, 79, 86, 87, 115
  Sabre-toothed 13, *14*
  Siberian 13, *14*, 15, *17*, 44, *54*, 62, *86*, 87, *101*, 113, 115
  Sumatran 13, *54*, 86, 87, 115
Tiger Ecology Project 38–41, *44*, 50
Tiger Task Force 91
Tigers, description of 12, 15, 16–17, 23
  food of, and eating *24*, 25–31, *108*, *109*, *111*
  geographical ranges of 13, 15, *16*, *17*
  habitat of 15, 16, 77
  hunting methods of *10*, 17, 25, 32–7, 58
  longevity of 53, 56
  man-eating by *26*, 59–67
  numbers of 56, 65, 68, 80, 82–7, 108, 115
  poaching of *76*, *77*, *98*, 108, 115
  poisoning of 75, *76*, *77*
  reactions towards man 12, 60
  reproduction of 50, 51–6
  response to water *21*, 23, *32*, 65, 67
  scent-marking by *44*, 45–6, 50, 51
  shooting of 68, *70*, *73*, *76*
  territorial behaviour of 37–45, 67
  tracking of 82, *83*
  trade in skins of 62, 75, 76, *77*, 86, 103–5
  trapping of 75, *76*
  vocalizations of 46–50
  weights and measurements of 15
  white 22–3
Tigress, behaviour of 40, *44*
  education of cubs by 53, 56–9, *89*
  gestation period of 51
  litter sizes of 51–2, 53
  mortality of cubs 52, 53, *55*, *89*
  reproductive potential of 46, 51, 53, 56
  territory of 40–2
Tipu, Sultan, of Mysore 90
Tourism 12, *36*, 101
Turkey 15, 86

Udaipur, Maharajah of 70
Umed Singh, Prince of Kotah *73*
United Nations 92, 108
USSR 16, 76, 80, 86, 114
Uttar Pradesh 62, 75

Vietnam, War in 25, 62, 79, 114
Vultures 25, *29*, 75

Wangchuh, H.M. King Jigme Singh-ye 111
Wapiti, Manchurian 44, *86*
William of Gloucester, H.R.H. Prince 70
World Conservation Strategy 7
World Wildlife Fund 7, 8, 9, 38, 67, 79, 81, 82, 89, 91, 92, 93, 94, 96, 101, 103, 104, 105, 113

Yak 94

Zambia 101
Zoological Society of London 46, *54*
Zoos 22, 51, 52, 53, *54*, 58, 85